Creating Space
without
Adding On

Creating Space without Adding On

Jack P. Jones

TAB Books
Division of McGraw-Hill, Inc.
Blue Ridge Summit, PA 17294-0850

FIRST EDITION
FIRST PRINTING

© 1993 by **Jack P. Jones**
Published by TAB Books.
TAB Books is a division of McGraw-Hill, Inc.

Library of Congress Cataloging-in-Publication Data

Jones, Jack Payne, 1928-
    Creating space without adding on / by Jack P. Jones.
      p.   cm.
    Includes index.
    ISBN 0-8306-3958-6   ISBN 0-8306-3959-4 (pbk.)
    1. Dwellings—Remodeling—Amateurs' manuals. I. Title.
TH4816.J645 1993
643'.7—dc20   92-34048
                                    CIP

Acquisitions Editor: Kimberly Tabor
Editorial team: Debra Marshall, Editor
              Lori Flaherty, Managing Editor
Production team: Katherine G. Brown, Director of Production
              Lisa M. Mellott, Layout
              Rhonda E. Baker, Typesetting
              Jana L. Fisher, Typesetting
              Ollie Harmon, Typesetting
              Lisa M. Mellott, Typesetting
              Brenda M. Plasterer, Typesetting
              Kelly S. Christman, Proofreading
              Joann Woy, Indexing
              Marty Ehrlinger, Computer Illustrator
              Stephanie Myers, Computer Illustrator
Design team: Jaclyn J. Boone, Designer
            Brian Allison, Associate Designer
Cover design: Holberg Design, York, Pa.
Cover photograph: Brent Blair   TAB3

For Kimberly Whittle

Contents

13 Skylights 227

Chapter 1

Introduction

Where will it end? Housing costs for new and used homes increase daily. What is the increase in the median price for a house today compared to last year or the year before? Is it 2 percent, 5 percent, or greater? How much will the price of the same house increase by next year, or the next? Many of us can remember when $12,500 bought a new, well-designed three-bedroom brick veneer structure in a choice area.

Living space is at an all-time premium. Homeowners spend more than $25 billion a year on do-it-yourself projects to improve their homes. Many gain habitable space without adding more rooms. They "build up" instead of "move up" and so avoid financial burdens (and risks).

A house is a box containing a number of smaller boxes we call rooms. It has always been expensive to add a box, and is even more so now. If you need the extra room and have the money and space on your lot to build an addition, do it. Call a few building contractors and get bids. Let a builder handle the worry and the work.

But it will cost you a bundle.

A contractor is in business to make a profit. In addition to the cost of materials and labor, taxes and insurance comprise 19 to 29 percent of the cost of the job. Another 22 to 28 percent will be charged to overhead. All this is spent before the contractor makes a profit. Guess who has to pay for it?

Forget the contractor; hire a carpenter. Not much overhead, taxes, or other money-gobblers there; a carpenter hired by the hour will cut expenses considerably. The savings go into your pocket, and you retain the responsibility for the job: planning, ordering materials, dealing with mistakes, and so on. A person hired by the hour is only responsible for doing what he or she is instructed to do, i.e., remove a wall, build a wall, etc.

There has been an explosion of activity in basement and attic conversions and this is where we will be spending a lot of our time. These are big do-it-yourself (DIY) projects requiring a lot of planning and a tremendous amount of work. If you are inclined to be impatient, lazy, or easily sidetracked, put this book down and go get a simpler hobby.

The next couple hundred pages or so are designed as a roadmap to guide you through the obstacles most do-it-yourselfers face when beginning a major building adventure—or misadventure.

Don't let anyone misguide you. There is no simple way to build anything. Driving a nail requires a certain technique, and many carpenters will swear it is an art.

LEARN BEFORE YOU LEAP

Don't make the mistake of jumping into a project without giving the matter the thought and study it requires. Removing or relocating a wall requires some thought. You don't want the ceiling and roof sinking dangerously downward. There is an important difference between the function and purpose of a load-bearing wall and a non-load-bearing partition.

Many homeowners believe you must have some building experience before tackling the projects covered in this book. It's true that there is nothing like experience, but many conversion projects are successfully completed by people who have no experience. What these people have in common, however, is that they take the time to find answers.

Leaping is when you spend 80 hours of back-breaking work and a thousand dollars to relocate a partition 2 feet from its original position. *Learning* is realizing that a two-foot gain in floor space is never worth the trouble and expense involved.

In the pages ahead you will learn something about design shifting (floor plan modification), building materials, conversion possibilities, major do's and don'ts, computing labor hours, and you will receive step-by-step instructions.

AVOIDING COSTLY MISTAKES

The only way to avoid mistakes is to think your project through. When planning to enlarge a room by removing a partition, begin by envisioning the larger room, the placement of furniture, traffic flow, activities that take place in the room, and the cost of making a change. Will the added space serve the purpose?

Second, what space will you sacrifice to gain the larger room? Will you lose a room? Will the change increase the value of your home?

Third, can you do the project yourself? Is the partition a load-bearing wall? Have you considered what steps are necessary to brace the structure when removing a supporting wall?

There are many details to consider when redesigning or converting space. Failure to carefully consider each detail can result in costly mistakes. Take your time. Get professional advice when you have doubts. You can make the project a pleasure or a nightmare.

Most DIY projects require a building permit. A basement or attic conversion requires a permit. Relocating, adding, or removing a wall usually requires a permit. Your local code probably reads:

"It shall be unlawful for any person, firm or corporation to erect, construct, enlarge, alter, repair, move, improve, convert, or demolish any building or structure . . . without first obtaining a permit."

Extremely restrictive, isn't it? But there are exemptions. You would not need a permit to replace kitchen cabinets, change a door, or redo your floor covering. Neither would a permit be required for normal repair and maintenance.

If you are planning to convert your attic or basement, or even just a portion, you should consult your building department. An inspection of the premises might be required before a permit can be issued. There could be other restrictions applicable to your neighborhood. Avoid a costly mistake and check the laws before investing time and money. In a planning stage, you'll:

- Decide that additional habitable space is needed.
- Determine where the space can be obtained.
- Determine the structural worthiness of area.
- Decide if you can do the work.
- Itemize work that must be left to professionals (such as electrical, plumbing, and tile setting).
- Schedule time and days to do the work.
- Estimate the cost of the project.
- Estimate the hours needed.
- Make financial arrangements.

BEATING THE HIGH COST OF ADDING SPACE

If you have room, adding onto your house can be a solution. If additions are permitted, in most cases you will find that the only place to expand the house is at the back. A septic tank, underground lines, and pipes can further restrict the placement of your addition.

Addition work is new construction, and as such, outrageously expensive. Depending on your neighborhood, an addition could be "overbuilding." That is, putting more money into your home than you could sell it for. If the houses on your street are valued at $30,000 and you spend $12,000 to add a room to yours, you will never sell the place for enough to get your money back.

To minimize your loss, the less you have to invest to gain much needed space, the better. Redesigning or converting space can give you a great deal more value for your dollar and can increase the worth of your home.

STRUCTURAL FLAWS AND INSPECTION GUIDELINES

The time to find structural flaws or determine remedial construction needs is during the planning stage, before you start actually building. Building materials are expensive: you want every board and nail to count for something, to provide the most space for the least number of dollars.

Regardless of when your home was built, its construction probably followed the codes in place at the time and adhered to existing standard construction practices, I say "probably" because not all houses are constructed by competent or honest builders. Let's look at what you should search for when planning to convert space.

If you plan to convert basement space, FIG. 1-1 lists some of the major things to look for. A dry basement was constructed properly. A wet basement was not. Don't put time, money, and effort into remodeling a basement with serious flaws; a basement that is always damp is not suitable for habitation.

I-I A basement inspection list helps pinpoint problems.

Basement Inspection Guide

1. Size of Basement
   Length_____
   Width_____
   Total square feet (L × W)_____
2. Ceiling height_____
   (Measure from floor to bottom of floor joists. Minimum height required: 6'9")
3. Floor
   Concrete_____
   Wood_____
   Other_____
4. Walls
   Concrete_____
   Masonry block_____
   Other_____
5. Ceiling
   Finished_____
   Unfinished_____
6. Windows
   Number_____
   Size_____

NOTE: Most codes provide that every habitable room shall have at least one window or skylight facing directly to the outdoors which can be easily opened, or such other device as will ventilate the room. The total of openable window area in every habitable room shall equal to at least forty-five (45) percent of the minimum window area size or minimum skylight-type window size, as required, or shall have other approved, equivalent ventilation . . . Year round mechanically ventilating conditioned air systems may be substituted for windows except in rooms used for sleeping purposes.

The window size in a basement is important. Every room used for sleeping, living, or dining must have at least two means of egress, at least one of which shall be a door or stairway providing a means of unobstructed travel to the outside at ground level.

Each sleeping room, unless it has two doors providing separate means of escape, or has a door leading outside of the building directly, shall have at least one outside window which can be opened from the inside without the use of tools, with sill height not more than 44 inches above the floor, providing not less than 5.7 square feet of openable area and no net clear opening dimension less than 24 inches in height and 20 inches in width.

7. Outside entrance

  Existing_____
  Planned_____

8. Furnace type

  Gas_____
  Liquid fuel_____
  Other_____

NOTE: Check code before enclosing furnace in a separate room. Size of enclosure will depend upon furnace size, fuel burned, and air supply required for combustion.

9. General condition

  Water present_____
  Walls damp_____
  Floor damp_____
  Surface water enters basement_____
  Water proofing needed_____
  Walls cracked_____
  Floor cracked_____

10. Sump pump

  Installed_____
  Planned_____

11. Finish grade

  Acceptable for conversion_____
  Requires excavating_____

NOTE: Some codes provide that the average finish grade elevation at exterior walls shall not be more than 48 inches above finish floor of a habitable room. This does not apply to basement recreation rooms not intended for year round occupancy, bathrooms, storage or utility rooms. Where the finish grade is irregular, calculate areas separately to obtain average height.

1-1 Continued.

Basement dampness comes from two sources: water seepage and condensation. When water comes up through the floor or through the walls, the basement is leaking. Condensation is caused by the basement's interior air (comparatively warm and humid) hitting the cool masonry basement walls. Chapter 9 discusses how to solve these and other problems.

Figure 1-2 lists those items to look for when planning an attic conversion. Figure 1-3 identifies key roof framing components. Attic space offers many opportunities for the do-it-yourselfer. For example, an attic can be converted to a child's bedroom with plenty of play room.

Attic Inspection Guide

1. Type construction
   Gable_____   Pitch_____
   Hip_____   Pitch_____
2. Rafters
   Conventional_____
   Truss_____
   Type_____
3. Floor joists
   2 × 6, 16" OC_____
   2 × 6, 24" OC_____
   2 × 8, 16" OC_____
   2 × 8, 24" OC_____
   Other_____
4. Floor joist span_____
5. Flooring
   None_____
   Boards_____
   Plywood_____
   OSB_____
   NOTE: Flooring must be removed if floor joists reinforcement is required.
6. Floor Insulation
   Type_____
   Thickness_____
7. Rafters
   2 × 6, 16" OC_____
   2 × 6, 24" OC_____
   2 × 8, 16" OC_____
   2 × 8, 24" OC_____
8. Bracing
   Diagonal_____
      Spacing_____
   "Trough"_____
   Purlin_____
   Collar_____
      Spacing_____
   Other_____
9. Roof sheathing
   Board_____
   Plywood_____
   OSB_____
10. Windows
    Number_____
    Size_____
    Location
       Gable_____
       Dormer_____

1-2 A properly prepared attic inspection list can prevent costly mistakes.

11. Dormers

    Number_____

    Type

        Shed_____

        Gable_____

    Location

        Front_____

        Back_____

    Ceiling height_____

    Width_____

12. Attic headroom

    To collar_____

    To ridge (peak)_____

    To proposed ceiling_____

13. Knee Wall Data

    Height_____

    Recommended height

        5'_____

        4'6"_____

        4'_____

    Available floor space

        With 5' wall_____

        With 4'6" wall_____

        With 4' wall_____

14. Stairway

    None_____

    Inadequate_____

    Adequate_____

    Outside entrance_____

15. Chimney

    Masonry_____

        Size_____

    Metal_____

        Size_____

    Location

        Center of attic_____

        At end_____

        At side_____

16. Electrical

    Light fixtures_____

        Type

            Pull chain_____

            Switch operated_____

    Receptacles_____

    Circuits_____

    Additional circuits required_____

    Cable runs

        On top of framing_____

        Under floor joists_____

        Along side floor joists_____

        Underside of rafters_____

NOTE: Wiring on room side of structural components must be re-routed.

17. How will I get building materials to the attic?
   By outside stairway_____
   Through window_____
   Through opening cut in gable_____
18. Will I need scaffolding to do the job?
   (Steel scaffold comes in sections providing a 4-foot-high platform. A 16-foot-high platform is obtained by joining 4 sections or "jacks.")
19. Can a truck drive close enough to house to hoist materials to attic level?
   NOTE: Trucks or heavy equipment should not operate within 10 feet of basement areas.

1-2 Continued.

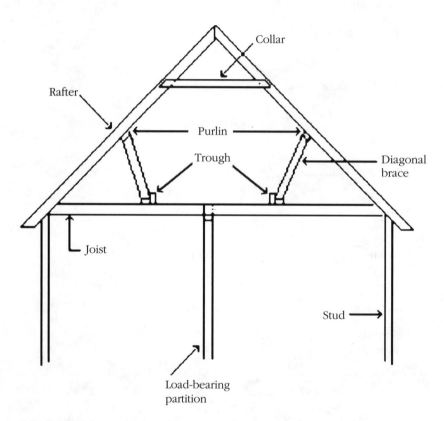

1-3 Framing the conventional way.

Unfinished attics can become extremely hot so ventilation is essential even when working on mild days. Plan how you will get building materials into the attic. Will you need outside scaffolding and a second-story entrance to bring framing lumber and 4-x-8-foot panels to the attic? If the attic is a gable type and has windows, you're in luck. Few attics, however, have large windows. Attics in modern hip roof structures are commonly low and of insufficient height to convert. We will take a detailed look at attics you can convert in Chapter 10.

Chapter **2**

Interior wall framing

Interior walls can be load-bearing or non-load-bearing. In either case, the wall is a partition separating space. In *stick* or standard construction, the bearing wall is located toward the center of the building and perpendicular to the run of ceiling joists and rafters. Bearing walls reduce the span of ceiling joists, so shorter lumber can be used. Bearing walls provide structural support.

Roof trusses do not require a bearing wall; the truss spans the full width of the structure. In truss construction, interior walls might be used to support the lower chord of the truss when the wall is perpendicular to the truss and is secured to the chord.

If your home was built using trusses, you probably could remove any interior wall without being concerned about loads. Manufactured roof trusses are a fairly recent development in housing construction and their use is still not widespread in many areas. Figure 2-1 shows three popular truss types. Note the slope (pitch) of the roof is shown as 5/12, 2½/12, etc.

What is a wall frame? Is there a difference between the frame of an exterior (load-bearing) wall and a load-bearing interior wall? How does the frame of a non-load-bearing wall differ? How do you tie one wall to another?

Figure 2-2 shows exterior wall with a door and window opening. Exterior walls perpendicular to the run of ceiling joists and rafters are bearing walls. The end walls of gable roof construction are non-bearing walls.

Figure 2-3 shows an interior wall that could be either bearing or non-bearing, depending on its location. Figure 2-4 shows how a standard corner post is fashioned. Figure 2-5 illustrates how to tie an interior partition with an exterior wall using a Tee stud assembly. The terms "wall" and "partition" mean the same thing and are used interchangeably in this book.

STANDARD WALL CONSTRUCTION

The standard wall is framed with 2 × 4s. It begins with a bottom plate, called a sole plate. The studs rest on the sole plate in the upright position.

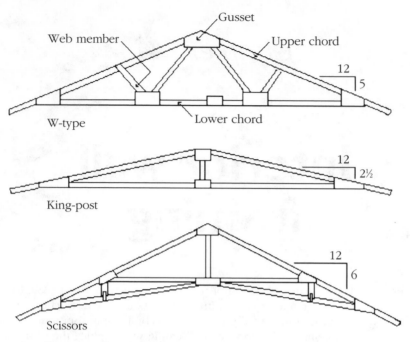

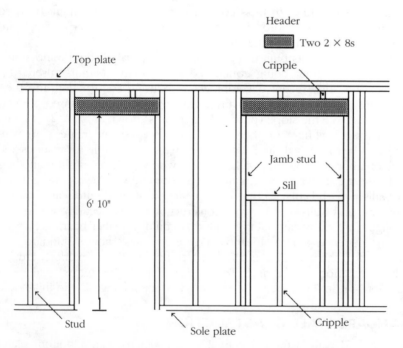

2-1 Three varieties of light wood trusses.

2-2 Exterior load-bearing wall with door and window openings.

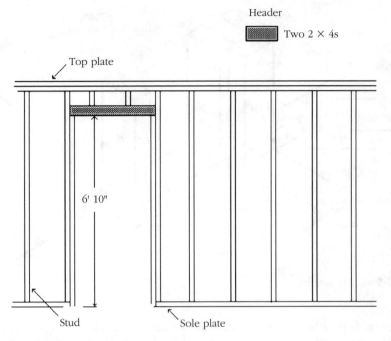

2-3 Interior wall with door opening.

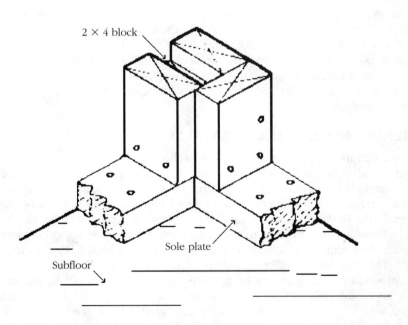

2-4 Using three studs and blocks to build a standard corner stud assembly.

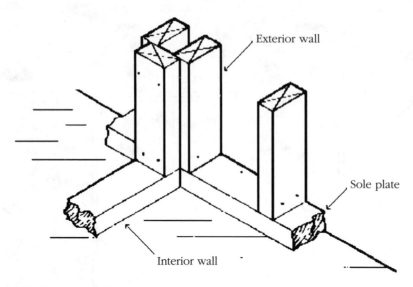

Exterior wall

Sole plate

Interior wall

2-5 T stud assembly.

The studs may be spaced 16 or 24 inches on center. The studs are capped with a top plate, usually consisting of a doubled 2 × 4. Interior and exterior walls are framed in the same manner.

The interior wall may be finished with many materials. Gypsum board, commonly called wallboard, is widely used. Wallboard may be painted or covered with wallpaper. Prefinished wood panels are also popular. Wallboard, paneling and similar "dry" sheets are referred to as drywall, distinguished from plaster, which must be applied wet.

Plaster, a widely-used smooth finish up until about the late forties, lost out in popularity to the more economical drywall materials. Plaster is still used, however, in some homes, and brick, stone, logs, tile, glass, and other materials are often used in interior walls, either as structural or decorative finishes.

REMOVING LOAD-BEARING WALLS

Not all bearing walls are straight—the wall may jog in or out a short distance and continue its run. Removing any wall requires planning. Before beginning the task of doing away with a bearing wall you must temporarily brace it; FIG. 2-6 shows how. Lay a 2 × 4 or larger member on the floor, perpendicular to the floor joist run, to evenly distribute the load of the bracing.

There are several ways to provide permanent support for ceiling joists affected by removing the bearing wall. First, let's take off the finish material.

The removal of wall materials is demolition work. You may wish to save wood paneling and molding, particularly old-style molding that may be impossible to match. Use care when removing any trim and paneling you want to save; a flat tool such as a wide-blade chisel, putty knife or flat pry bar works well when loosening trim, wood panel and boards.

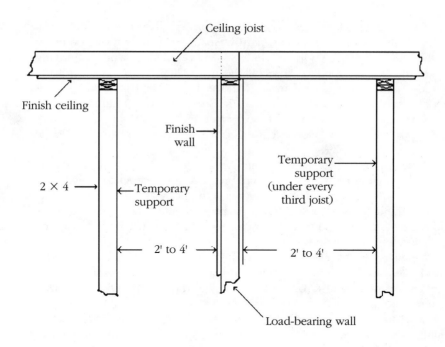

Ceiling joist

Finish ceiling

Finish wall

Temporary support (under every third joist)

2 × 4

Temporary support

2' to 4'

2' to 4'

Load-bearing wall

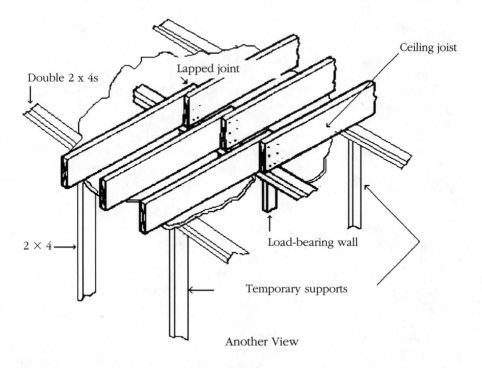

Double 2 x 4s

Lapped joint

Ceiling joist

2 × 4

Load-bearing wall

Temporary supports

Another View

2-6 Brace well before removing load-bearing walls.

Plaster may be loosened and cracked into small pieces by tapping it with a hammer. Use a crow bar, narrow spade, or similar tool to remove firmly attached plaster. Open windows for ventilation when removing plaster. It's a dusty job, so close off the rest of the house to control the spread of dust. Wear a dust mask. Remove the plaster lath, using a hammer and pry bar for wood and metal lath. Below this is the framing.

Now remove any wiring or pipe located in the wall—but do not fool around with electricity. House current can kill! Cut the power off at the main panel.

If the wiring end-runs (stops) into a wall receptacle or light fixture via the top or bottom plate, you need only remove the receptacle or light fixture, push the loose wire back underneath the floor or back into the attic. Remove the surplus wire. Run the end into a junction box, cap the wires with wire nuts, and tape with electrical tape, firmly securing the nut to the wire. Install the cover on the box.

Wiring making a circuit run into and beyond a receptacle or fixture must be removed from the partition and rejoined at another location.

Remove pipes and reroute them to rejoin the system. Old galvanized pipe may be replaced with (easy to work with) PVC pipe.

Now, to remove a load-bearing partition you must first support the ceiling joists. If the attic space above the partition is roomy enough to work in, a supporting beam can be installed above the ceiling joists in the attic and the joists supported from the beam as shown in FIG. 2-7. Use three 16d nails to tie the joists together. Secure the 1 × 4 to the joist and bracket with four 8d nails. Metal strap may be used in lieu of wood brackets. (FIG. 2-8.)

Use care when removing framing members. A cat's claw is a good tool for removing nails from framing. Use a crow bar to loosen and remove members such as the bottom and top plates. Protruding nails in dismantled wood and wallboard are dangerous. Make it a practice to remove all nails from material as you proceed with the demolition.

The support beam must be supported on each end by exterior walls, a bearing partition, or a post that will transfer the load to the foundation.

(How will you get the beam material into the attic? Can a window be opened or a vent removed to provide access to long lumber from the outside?)

Note in FIG. 2-7 that the joists are attached to the beam at the point of joist overlap. Temporary supports are not necessary when you install the beam above the joists and lock it all together as shown.

The exposed beam solves the cavity problem in the ceiling when a wall is removed. Install temporary supports as shown in FIG. 2-6. Remove the partition, install the beam, and remove the temporary supports. Make sure there is a minimum of 6'8" between the bottom of the beam and the floor. Figure 2-9 illustrates exposed beam placement. Toenail each ceiling joist to the beam with two 8d nails.

Support the beam at each end with upright 2 × 4s (cripple) to carry the load to the foundation. To fit the beam into a saddle support within

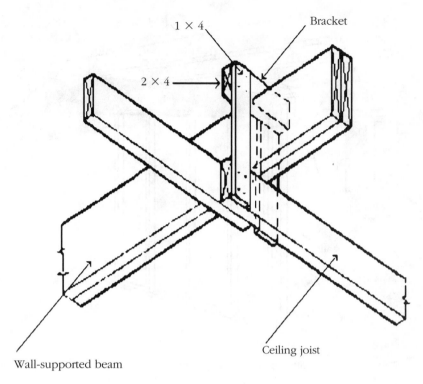

2-7 Installing supporting beam in attic above the ceiling joists.

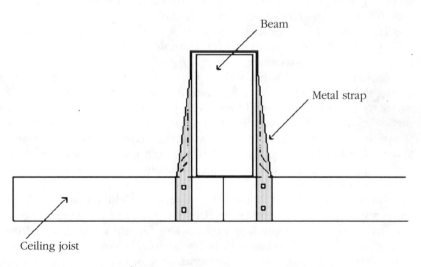

2-8 Use metal strap to support ceiling joists by beam in attic.

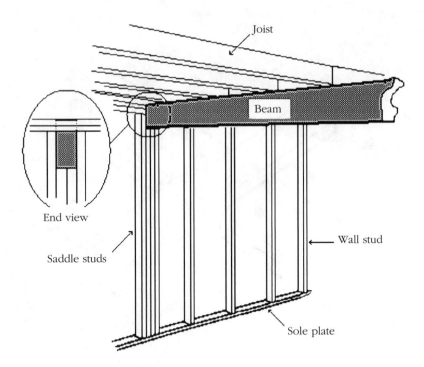

2-9 Install a beam fitted into a saddle to support ceiling joist after removing wall.

the wall's plane as seen in FIG. 2-9, you may elect to use one or two 2×4s for the cripple, shown in FIG. 2-10 and FIG. 2-11. Use 12d nails spaced 16 inches apart and staggered to fabricate the saddle members. Toenail the unit to the bottom and top plates with 8d nails.

The exposed beam can be finished with the same materials as the wall or ceiling finish, or it may be left natural. You might prefer to enclose the beam with wood paneling.

An exposed beam is not always the answer. In cases where a flush ceiling is desired and no attic space is available (as in a first floor of a two-story house), a reinforced beam might be the solution; see FIG. 2-12. If this is your method, place temporary supports in place, as described above, before removing the bearing wall. The ceiling joists must be cut to allow room for the beam. The ends of the beam must be supported by a wall or post carrying the load to the foundation. Install joist hangers to secure the joists to the beam.

The beam span, span of joists butting into it, and the material used for the beam will determine the beam size. The width of the joists often dictate (as in our second-story house) the width (depth) of the material used in the beam. A steel-reinforced beam can ensure adequate structural support provided the steel is of the proper thickness. Bolt the beam together, the steel sandwiched between the wood members. The steel sold for this purpose comes with pre-drilled bolt holes.

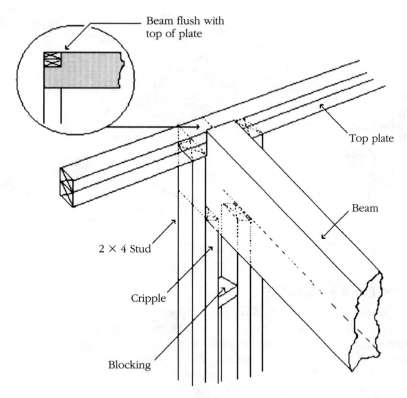

Beam flush with
top of plate

Top plate

Beam

2 × 4 Stud

Cripple

Blocking

2-10 Saddle construction using two cripples.

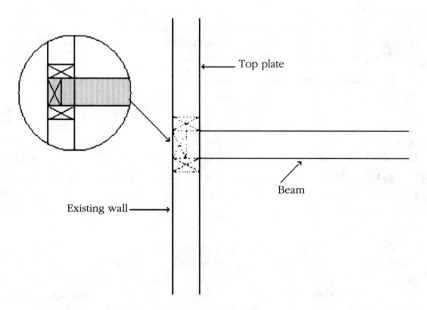

Top plate

Beam

Existing wall

2-11 Plan view of single cripple supporting beam in a saddle.

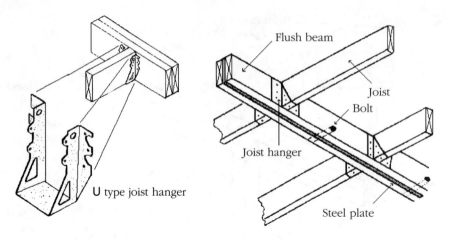

2-12 Flush beam reinforced with steel plate.

BEAM TYPE AND SIZES

You can make your own built-up beam by spiking two or more pieces of lumber together. You can strengthen the beam by spreading wood glue between the members and clamping tightly before nailing. For built-up beams with three or more members, face-nail along each side with 20d nails spaced 32 inches apart and staggered.

Arriving at the correct size beam for the span and load can be tricky. For most home projects, two 2 × 12s nailed together with 10d nails staggered at 20 inches can handle normal loads up to 12 feet. Different span limitations are imposed, however, if the beam must support, say, a load-bearing wall in the story above; in that case a beam of three 2 × 12s might be required. A solid 6 × 10 manufactured glue-laminated beam will support longer spans under heavier loads.

Solid laminated wood beams Before the arrival of glue-laminated construction, the sizes of the solid saw timbers available limited heavy timber construction. Laminated beams now enable construction of buildings with large unobstructed areas—like gymnasiums and warehouses. If you need a beam that could span the entire width of your house, a solid laminated beam is available for almost any combination of span and load.

Solid wood beams Solid wood beams are what the name implies. Use care to select a beam that is straight and not warped or twisted. The longer the span, the larger the beam must be to handle the load, and the higher its cost.

Laminated truss beams The laminated truss beam consists of a top and bottom chord with spaced short members joining the two. Both sides (width) of the beam is formed by plywood. The beam's strength is due to the combination of suitably thick plywood or OSB panels and lumber (2 × 4s, 2 × 6s, etc.) glue-nailed together in a rectangular truss. The truss beam is used for floor joists, ceiling joists, girders and beams.

Steel beams Many basement girders are steel I-beams. For long spans, steel is ideal. Steel beams can be boxed and attractively finished.

Other beams Innovation in the construction industry continues to create new materials for building. Laminated veneer lumber is available in 1 ply 1¾ × 9¼ to 18 inch widths for spans up to 26 feet. These high-quality, wood products are designed to eliminate the common problems of solid wood products. They're stronger, longer, more stable, and easier to handle.

REMOVING NON-LOAD-BEARING WALLS

A non-bearing partition is removed in much the same manner as a load-bearing wall except that you do not have to support the ceiling joists. A wall serving as a mere partition supports only itself. Such walls commonly run parallel to the ceiling joists.

Whenever a wall, whether it be bearing or nonbearing, is removed, a cavity is left in the ceiling, floor and walls. In plaster or sheetrock walls and ceilings the problem is not difficult: plaster can be spread in the cavity, finished smooth, and feathered to hide any evidence of the wall's removal. In plasterboard walls and ceilings, cut drywall of the same thickness to fit the cavity and tape and cement it in with joint compound. Feather the seams.

Where wood strip flooring is laid parallel to the dismantled wall, strips of the same thickness can be installed in the cavity. The added flooring strips are then sanded and finished to match the existing floor.

If the flooring is laid perpendicular to the cavity, your patchwork of short flooring pieces placed in the gap will have to be outstanding to escape even the casual eye. A new floor covering is usually the best solution. Fill the cavity with same-size wood strips, plywood, or OSB to make the floor a ready base for new flooring. Your patchwork must be flush with the floor and all cracks filled to avoid showing through resilient flooring.

The ends of the wood strip flooring laid perpendicular to the wall you removed will be uneven. Measure the cavity at the widest width and transfer the measurement to each end of the cavity. Snap a chalk line at both sides of the cavity, making sure the distance between the line is the same at both ends and squared with the room (see FIG. 2-13). Saw along the chalk lines with the blade of the power saw set to the thickness of the flooring strips. Use a nail-cutting blade. Always protect your eyes by wearing safety goggles.

ADDING A PARTITION

Many older homes have large rooms. Some have bedrooms 16 × 14 feet or larger. To add a bathroom and closet in a 16 × 14 room, you must construct partitions. Erecting a partition does not create space: it merely changes the function of existing space, so you need to get as much out of the change as possible. A partition can turn an oversize room into a guest room with private bath and increased closet space. Or, it might become the new master bedroom you've always wanted.

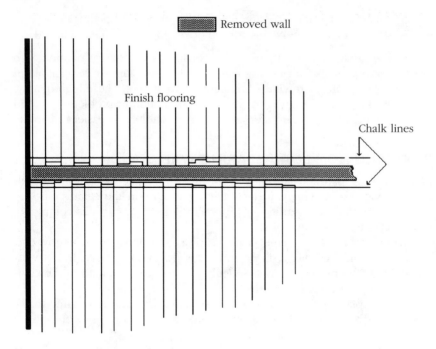

 Removed wall

Finish flooring

Chalk lines

2-13 Mark and saw uneven boards.

Room layout Figure 2-14 shows one way to lay out the room for partitions for a closet and bath. The important thing is to get the rooms as square as possible. Establish points A and B 5 feet from the wall and snap chalk line A-B. Measure 4 feet from the wall and snap line C-D. Line E-F is marked 4 feet from line C-D. Allow 3½ inches for the thickness of the framing plus the thickness of the finish walls. You'll need 5 feet clearance between the framing for the length of a standard bath tub. A full bath requires a toilet, lavatory, and a tub or shower. Arrange each for easy and comfortable use. Figure 2-15 gives minimum spacing for fixtures.

Figure 2-16 provides more information on bathroom fixture placement. Placing cabinets over a toilet does not change the toilet's installation dimensions.

Intersecting walls tie-in There are several ways to position tie-in members of a frame wall. Tie-in A, FIG. 2-17 is possible when the existing wall is not finished in the area of the tie-in. The Tee is made and nailed into place in the existing wall. Tie-in B is preferable when the existing wall is finished. There is no need to nail the frame of the added partition to the existing wall. The added partition merely supports itself, and is secured at the top and bottom; further anchoring is not necessary.

A simple way to position members for a tie-in of a wall added as an ell is shown in C and D as a left and a right turn. The configuration provides good stability and plenty of nailing space to attach finish materials.

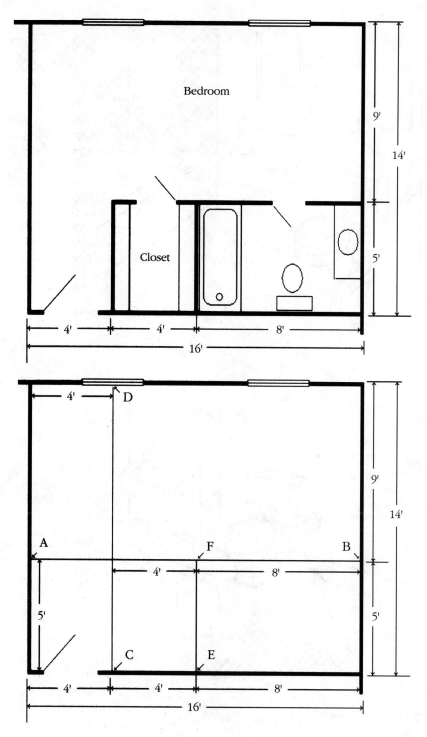

2-14 Marking the room for adding partitions.

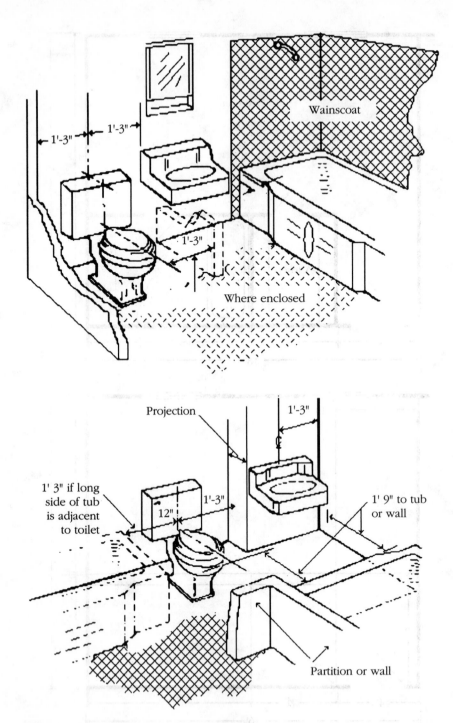

2-15 Workable dimensions for fixture placement.

Labels within the figure:

Wainscoat

1'-3" 1'-3"

1'-3"

Where enclosed

Projection

1'-3"

1' 3" if long side of tub is adjacent to toilet

12" 1'-3"

1' 9" to tub or wall

Partition or wall

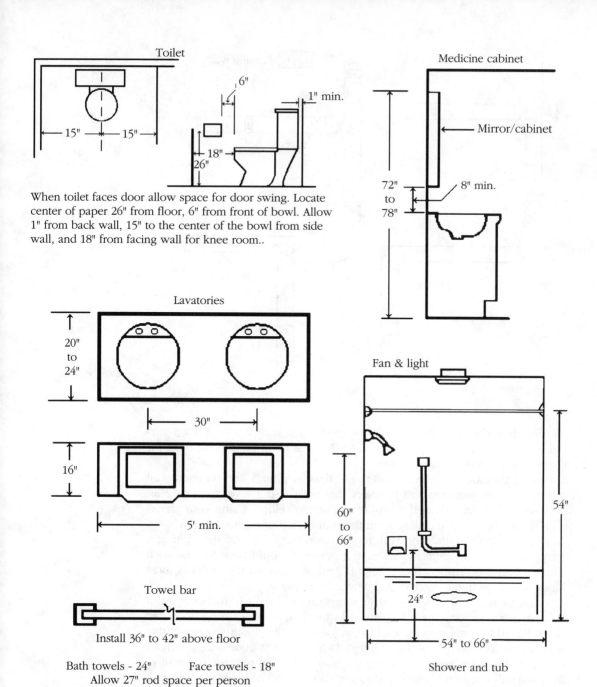

Toilet

When toilet faces door allow space for door swing. Locate center of paper 26" from floor, 6" from front of bowl. Allow 1" from back wall, 15" to the center of the bowl from side wall, and 18" from facing wall for knee room..

Medicine cabinet

Mirror/cabinet

Lavatories

Towel bar

Install 36" to 42" above floor

Bath towels - 24"   Face towels - 18"
Allow 27" rod space per person

Fan & light

Shower and tub

2-16 Dimension guidelines for installing bathroom fixtures.

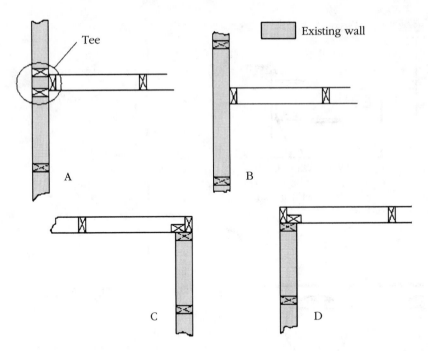

2-17 Intersecting walls tie-in.

Building the wall Most partitions are framed with 2 × 4s. A 2 × 3 partition works well when space is scarce. A 2 × 2 partition can be built for closets, saving more critical space.

Once the floor is marked (FIG. 2-14), draw a plumb line on each wall where the new partition will intersect that wall. Use a level to ensure an accurate plumb line. Mark the wall from floor to ceiling. Using your chalkbox, snap a line on the ceiling from the plumb line of each wall.

Forget about putting the wall together on the floor and then lifting it into place; for this method to work, the partition would have to be ½ inch shorter than the finished room height. And, damage to the walls is most likely when the frame is tilted and worked into place.

Instead, nail down the sole plate, staggering 16d nails 16 inches apart. It is always nice to have the sole plate fall directly over an existing floor joist when the added wall runs parallel to the joists, but it seldom works out that way, so you can do one of three things: 1) If it is a first floor wall, go under the floor and add a joist or blocking under the plate; 2) relocate the wall so the plate will rest over a joist or, 3) forget about it and nail the plate in place where you planned the wall. Most houses have sufficiently thick subfloors and underlayment to support the weight of a framed, non-load-bearing wall.

Nail up the top plate next. The plate needs to be secured solidly to the ceiling framing; this can present a problem if the partition is on the first floor of a two-story house and the finished ceiling is already in place. If the plate is directly under a ceiling joist or runs perpendicular to the ceiling joists, there will be no problem; just nail the plate to the member through the ceiling.

When the plate does not fall directly under a joist, do this: nail the end studs—the two that go against the walls where you marked the plumb line. If there is no stud in the existing wall to act as a nailer (a solid member to which another member can be nailed), cut the two end studs to fit on top of the sole plate and against the finished ceiling. (Before taking this step remove the crown and any other molding that might interfere with fitting the end studs); see FIG. 2-18.

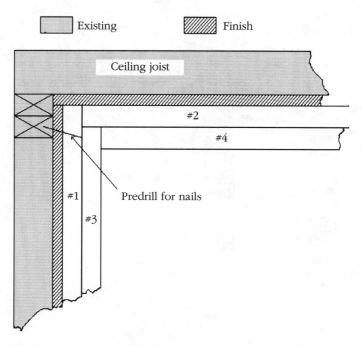

2-18 Framing for a non-load-bearing wall.

Toenail the end studs into the sole plate using 8d nails. Now pre-drill for 16d or larger nails to go through the end stud (#1) you just installed, to catch the top plate of the existing wall. Two nails are sufficient. Repeat these steps when installing the end stud on the other wall.

Cut the top plate (#2) to fit snugly between the end studs, firmly against the ceiling. (One continuous 2 x 4 is best for this member). Toenail the plate to #1 with 8d nails. Cement-coated "box" nails work well.

Now cut two jack studs (#3) to fit against the end studs, their ends butting firmly to the top plate (#2) to support it as shown in FIG. 2-18. Nail the jack stud to the top and sole plate with 8d nails and to the end stud with 12d or 10d nails, 16–20 inches apart.

Cut another 2 x 4 (#4), 3 inches shorter than the top plate (#2) and nail to the top plate with 12d nails. Your frame fit will look like FIG. 2-18.

In FIG. 2-19 your new partition is shown on the floor directly below the attic and you have access to the framing above the partition. The partition is located "between" the joist runs. It would be simpler to move the wall in or out to fall directly under a joist. The top plate could be nailed to the joist through the finish ceiling with 16d nails spaced 16 inches apart.

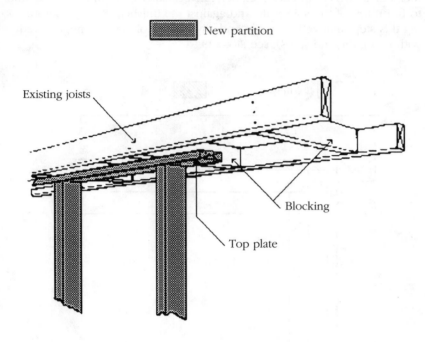

2-19 Nail top plate to blocking installed between existing ceiling joists.

Because the wall must be exactly where it is, do this: install solid blocking over the top plate area at no more than 2-foot spacing, and nail the top plate to each blocking with two 16d nails. If the ceiling and floor joists are perpendicular to the partition, nail the plates to each joists with two 16d nails.

Once the top and bottom plates are secured in place, install the studs, spacing them 16 or 24 inches on center. Fit the studs firmly in place, toe-nailing at each end with at least three 8d nails. Measure for the length for each stud. Floors and ceilings have a tendency to "wave," creating a height difference. A ¼-inch variation makes a big difference when fitting studs.

FRAMING OPENINGS

There are several ways to frame the doorway in your new wall. One method uses less material and saves a few dollars but makes a less sturdy wall. (The wall may shake when the door is closed firmly). The framing shown in FIG. 2-20 makes a solid opening. The opening height from the sub-floor to the bottom of the header is 6 feet 10 inches–6 feet 11 inches, depending on the thickness of the finish flooring. You may install a ⅜-inch spacer (plywood, OSB, etc.) between the header members, or leave the space clear.

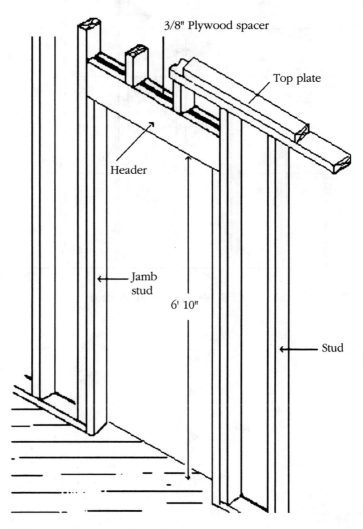

3/8" Plywood spacer

Top plate

Header

Jamb stud

6' 10"

Stud

2-20 A well-constructed opening.

A rule of thumb is that headers over openings 4 feet wide or smaller can be double 2 × 4s on edge. The common rule of thumb is: for every two feet of opening over four feet, increase the lumber size two inches. Thus, a four-foot opening requires doubled 2 × 4s on edge; six-foot openings need 2 × 6s; eight-foot openings, 2 × 8s, and ten-foot openings,

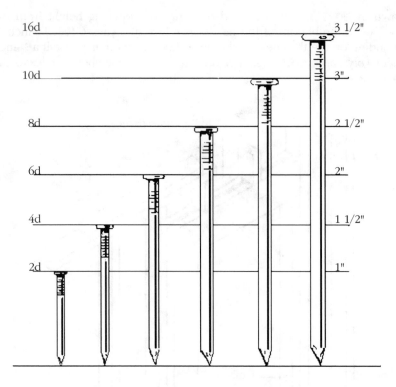

16d	3 1/2"
10d	3"
8d	2 1/2"
6d	2"
4d	1 1/2"
2d	1"

Nail Sizes & Number Per Pound

Size	Common	Box
4d	316	473
5d	271	406
6d	181	236
7d	161	210
8d	106	145
10d	69	94
12d	63	88
16d	49	71
20d	31	52
30d	24	46
40d	18	35

2-21 Nail size and quantity per pound.

2 × 10s. Headers must have the structural strength to support the load. As the size of the opening increases, so must the depth of the headers. Secure the header members to the studs with 16d nails.

I have referred to various nail sizes, and will continue to do so throughout the book; see FIG. 2-21. Nail sizes begin with 2d, which is 1 inch long and range up to 60d, which is 6 inches. The 2d–16d nails come in ¼ inch increments. Nails above 16d increase by ½ inch increments. Nails are distinguished by their heads, shanks, points, and surface finishes:

Bright After manufacture, nails are tumbled to remove chips and dirt, and packed uncoated.

Galvanized A zinc coating is applied by either the hot-tumbler method or electrolysis. The zinc coating protects against atmospheric corrosion.

Cement-coated To provide increased holding power, an adhesive is applied during the tumbler process.

Phosphate-coated A zinc-phosphate coating is applied to give some corrosion protection and holding capacity.

Blued Nails are sterilized by heating until an oxidation layer is formed.

Chapter **3**

Finishing
interior walls

Some of the best wall finishing, both in selection of materials and installation, is done by do-it-yourselfers. If you have spent time planning the redesign of space, removed or built a wall, you will be concerned about achieving the right finish. Perhaps it is a different look you are after—such as a wall or walls broken up with pilaster-type molding installed against a flat surface, as seen in FIG. 3-1.

Bassett Furniture Ind., Inc.

3-1 Adding elegance with vertical molding.

3-2 Wallboard is easily painted and maintained.

Drywall is an excellent finish for walls or ceilings. It also makes a good backing for prefinished plywood paneling, ceramic tile, wallpaper, etc. It is an ideal surface for interior paints. Drywall can be used to finish any room in a smooth, flat surface (see FIG. 3-2).

WALLBOARD

Wallboard is commonly referred to as drywall, the brand name sheetrock©, or just plain "rock" by many in the building trades. *Drywall* is an engineered panel made of gypsum (hydrated calcium sulfate) and other materials. The panel, or sheets, are finished on both sides with a durable paper. Several finishes are available, such as a plain manila paper face or with a factory-applied finish consisting of sheet vinyl or special printed paper. Sheets with aluminum foil reflective backing are also available. Drywall is noncombustible, nontoxic, dimensionally stable, and offers some resistance to sound transmission.

Drywall is available in several thicknesses and sizes. Install the ¼-inch thickness over old walls and ceilings or in sound-rated systems where the ¼-inch thickness is used in combination with other gypsum board to reduce through-the-wall sound transmission.

You can use the ⅜-inch thick panel for single-layer application over wall framing with members spaced no more than 16 inches on center (o.c.) I recommend using nothing less than ½-inch thick panels for a sturdier wall.

The spacing distance between studs, joists, and furring is important when hanging drywall. You can install ½-inch and ⅜-inch thicknesses vertically (with the long dimension parallel to the framing) when framing members are spaced 16 inches o.c. When installed horizontally (with the long dimension at right angles to the framing), the maximum spacing of framing members is 24 inches o.c.

Install either ½-inch or ⅝-inch drywall when the ceiling will support insulation or a water-based texture coating will be used. Install the ½-inch thickness horizontally over framing members spaced 16 or 24 inches o.c., or vertically over members spaced 16 inches o.c.

Coat the drywall with a pigmented primer-sealer before applying the textured coating, and do not install it in areas with continuous moisture or high humidity.

Wallboard is available in thicknesses of ¼, ⅜, ½ and ⅝ in widths of 16, 24, 32, and 48 inches, and in lengths from 4–16 feet in 1-foot increments. The 48 inch width is the most commonly used width for walls and ceilings. (Not all sizes are available in all thicknesses.)

INSTALLATION TECHNIQUES

Any 2 × 4 or larger framing will support wallboard. The finish wall will only be as straight as the framing behind it, however. If you used anything other than dry lumber for framing, you could cause a problem. Green lumber shrinks as it ages and could cause nails to pop out of the sheet rock. Also, green lumber has a tendency to twist and warp even after it is nailed in place. The four most common methods of hanging drywall are:

1. Nailing
2. Glue-nailing
3. "Floating angles"
4. Wood furring

Nailing Use the right nail, of proper length, to install drywall (see FIG. 3-3). For single nailing, follow the procedure detailed in FIG. 3-4.

Double nailing, shown in FIG. 3-5, minimizes nail pops. Start nailing at the center of the panel and work toward the edges, nailing the panel at intermediate studs 12 inches o.c. Space each pair of nails about 2 inches apart, as shown.

Glue-nailing Apply wallboard adhesive to framing member and allow to set; follow instructions of glue manufacturer. Then place the panel into position, and drive the minimum number of nails necessary to hold the panel in place until the glue dries. For example, for wall application space nails 24 inches o.c. For ceiling application, space nails 15 inches o.c. Figure 3-6 shows how to apply adhesive.

Floating angles This method will reduce the panel stress caused by frame settlement. Figures 3-7, 3-8 and 3-9 show the process.

Omit some of the nails at interior corners where ceiling and side walls meet and where side walls intersect. Nail as usual for the rest of the ceiling and wall area. Install the ceiling panels first, fitting the sheets snugly into all corners.

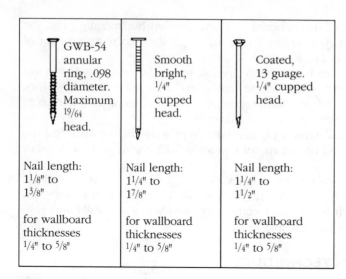

GWB-54 annular ring, .098 diameter. Maximum $^{19}/_{64}$ head.

Nail length: $1^1/_8$" to $1^3/_8$"

for wallboard thicknesses $^1/_4$" to $^5/_8$"

Smooth bright, $^1/_4$" cupped head.

Nail length: $1^1/_4$" to $1^7/_8$"

for wallboard thicknesses $^1/_4$" to $^5/_8$"

Coated, 13 guage. $^1/_4$" cupped head.

Nail length: $1^1/_4$" to $1^1/_2$"

for wallboard thicknesses $^1/_4$" to $^5/_8$"

3-3 Nails recommended for hanging wallboard.

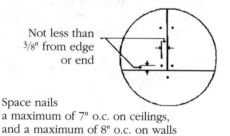

Not less than $^3/_8$" from edge or end

3-4 Wallboard single-nailing method.

Space nails a maximum of 7" o.c. on ceilings, and a maximum of 8" o.c. on walls

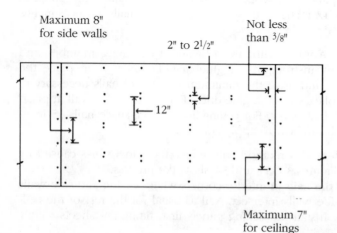

Maximum 8" for side walls

2" to $2^1/_2$"

Not less than $^3/_8$"

12"

3-5 Wallboard double-nailing method.

Maximum 7" for ceilings

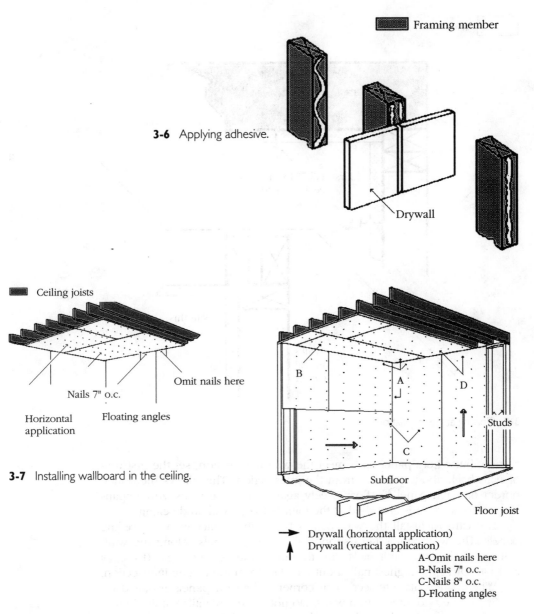

3-6 Applying adhesive.

Framing member

Drywall

Ceiling joists

Nails 7" o.c.

Omit nails here

Horizontal application

Floating angles

3-7 Installing wallboard in the ceiling.

B

A

D

Studs

C

Subfloor

Floor joist

→ Drywall (horizontal application)

↑ Drywall (vertical application)

A-Omit nails here
B-Nails 7" o.c.
C-Nails 8" o.c.
D-Floating angles

3-8 Side-wall installation details.

In horizontal ceiling applications use ordinary nailing procedures where the panel ends abut the wall intersection. Along the long edges of the panel, set back the first row of nails about 7 inches from the wall intersection.

When ceiling drywall is applied with long edges parallel to the joists, use ordinary nailing procedure where the long edges abut the wall inter-

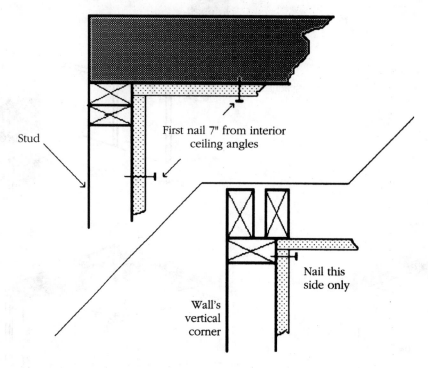

Wall board

Stud

First nail 7" from interior
ceiling angles

Nail this
side only

Wall's
vertical
corner

3-9 Floating angle installation.

section, but where panel ends meet the wall intersection, set the first row of nails back about 7 inches from the intersection. This allows the 7-inch border on each panel to "float" freely against the side walls. Any expansion or contraction is absorbed at the joint between wall and ceiling.

Use care to install the wall panels firmly in contact with the ceiling panels. The wall panels help support the ceiling panels. Along the wall-ceiling intersection, omit nails directly below the ceiling angle (FIGS. 3-8 and 3-9). Drive the highest nail about 7 inches from the ceiling intersection.

Where sidewalls intersect, omit corner-nailing on panels installed on the first of the two intersection walls. Do not drive any nails within 7 inches of the corner. Now hang the panels on the adjoining wall so they overlap the corner panels just applied. Nail the adjoining wall panels in the usual way. Space the nails 8 inches o.c., as depicted in FIG. 3-8.

Wood furring Wallboard installed on bowed, warped, or uneven ceiling joists will appear wavy. In other words, it will look awful. The solution is not to nail the wallboard to the joists; instead, nail 1 x 4 boards at right angles to the joists, shaving off the joist high spots and shimming the low spots where the furring and joists intersect. Pull a taut string across the bottom of the joists to find the high and low spots.

Space the furring boards 16 inches o.c. if the ceiling will support insulation. Otherwise the boards can be spaced 24 inches o.c. Nail the furring to each joist with two 8d nails. Apply the wallboard panels at right angles to the furring strips. Use the longest panels possible.

While it is possible for one person to nail 4 x 8 drywall in place on the ceiling, it's a gut-bender with side effects. I don't recommend it. But if you can't find a helper, use a T-brace. Make the brace by nailing a 2- or 3-foot 1 x 4 to a 2 x 4 one inch longer than the floor to ceiling height of your room. Use the T-brace to support the panel in place while you nail it. The brace is also helpful when two people are working with 4 x 8 or longer panels (see FIG. 3-10).

3-10 Using a T-brace to hold panels in place.

Nail setting When installing drywall, drive the nails so the heads are set slightly below the panel surface. Do not use a nail set—use a hammer. The head of the hammer will make a small "dimple". Do not break the paper face on the panel, drive the nails straight in, then fill nail dimples with joint cement. When cement is dry, sand it smooth. Repeat with second coat, if required.

Cementing and taping joints Cover joints between panels with a good coat of joint cement and tape. This is the first step to smoothing and leveling the wall surface. For good results:

- Start at the top of the wall (or beginning of joint in ceiling), using a 5-inch-wide spackling knife and spread the cement into the tapered edges of the joint, or between the gap (⅛") you left between the butt ends of the panels.
- Press tape into the recess until the joint cement is forced through the perforations. Use the 5-inch-wide spackling knife.

- Cover the tape with additional cement. Feather the edges.
- When the cement is dry apply a second coat, and feather the edges to extend beyond the edges of the first coat. Use a steel trowel for best results. If necessary, apply a third coat, feathering beyond second coat (see FIG. 3-11).

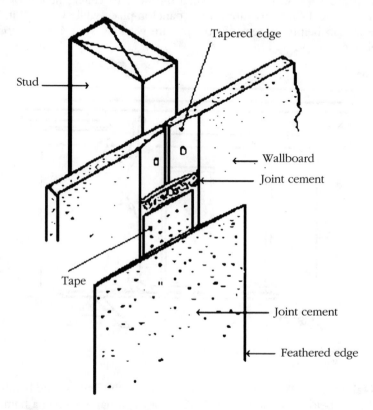

Tapered edge

Stud

Wallboard

Joint cement

Tape

Joint cement

Feathered edge

3-11 Using tape and joint compound to finish a wallboard seam.

- After the joint is dry, sand smooth. Do not sand the panel's paper coating.
- Finish interior corners with tape or molding. If you use tape, fold a strip of tape down the center to form a sharp angle (FIG. 3-12). Apply cement at the corner. Press the tape into place, and finish the corner with joint cement. When dry, sand corner smooth. Apply a second or third coat if necessary; feather the edges. Figure 3-13 shows an interior corner finished with molding. When molding is used, tape isn't necessary. Install metal corner beads on all outside corners. Cover the bead with joint cement.

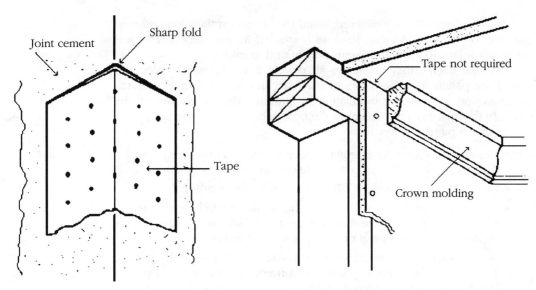

3-13 Installing molding at interior corner.

3-12 Spread cement and fold tape for corner fit.

How to cut drywall

Cut drywall with a sharp utility knife. Use a 4-foot straight edge to guide the blade. Here's how to make a professional cut:

- Cut completely through the face paper and into the core while holding the knife at right angles to the panel. Moderate pressure on the knife is all that is necessary. You do not have to cut through the panel.
- Break the panel at the cut by bending the smaller piece back. The panel will snap easily at the point cut.
- Using the utility knife, cut the paper on the panel back at the break.
- Make circular and square cut-outs with a keyhole or sabre saw.

WOOD AND HARDBOARD PANELS

Interior plywood and hardboard panels are 4 × 8 feet. Panels are finished to have the appearance of boards, of equal or random widths. Panels ¼ inch thick can be installed directly to studs spaced 24 inches o.c. Panels can also be applied directly to wallboard walls using glue and a few nails.

Plywood panels are made in a variety of wood species and finishes. Prices vary widely, depending on the species, the finish, and the quality. Hardboard panels printed with a wood-grain pattern are less expensive. High-quality hardboard paneling uses a photograph of wood to give the wood-grain effect. Thus, all the panels have the same wood-grain pattern. (Real wood panels all have different grain patterns.)

When the paneling is delivered, stand the sheets on their long edge in the area to be paneled for at least 48 hours before installation. This lets the panels adjust to the room's temperature and humidity.

Examine each panel to ensure all panels have the same color and tone. Even panels from the same lot may vary in color and texture. Match the grain and color before installation by standing the panels around the room. In this manner you can select the best pattern for the room.

To install panels, follow these steps:

- Measure floor to ceiling height at several points along the wall to detect variations. (Most walls will have some variation.)

- Cut each panel separately if height varies more than ½ inch.

- Cut each panel ½ inch shorter than the actual ceiling height (even when height varies more than half an inch). Floor and ceiling moldings will cover height variations up to 2 inches.

- Begin panel installation at a corner. Using a level, plumb the panel. The edge of the panel opposite the corner must center on a stud. Let's call this point *centered stud*.

- If the panel must be cut to fit, saw the side fitted to the corner. Measure for the cut from the centered stud to the corner. Also, check the measurements at the top and bottom of the wall from centered stud to corner.

- When cutting paneling with a power saw, cut from the panel's back. When cutting with a hand saw, cut from panel's finish side. This ensures cutting "into" the finish to avoid splintering. Use a fine tooth saw. Protect your eyes with safety goggles when using a power saw.

- Install the panel, using color-matching nails. Start nailing at a corner and move down the stud. Place edge nails 8–10 inches apart. Nail on intermediate studs the same way, spacing nails 8–10 inches apart.

- Never force panels into place. Their edges should lightly touch. Should the stud or backing wall show between panels edges (due to uneven panel edge), color the area of the stud with a black felt pen where the panels meet and install the panel.

- To cut out for a wall outlet, switch box, etc., measure from the floor up and from the edge of the previously installed panel. Transfer these measurements to the back of the panel to be cut. Careful: recheck the panel's position and the location of your cut. It is easy to become confused when transferring measurements to the back of the panel. Allow for the distance the panel will be off the floor.

Another method for marking cut-outs is to mark the front edge of the wall box with pencil or chalk; place the panel in place on the wall in the exact position it will be installed. Bump the panel firmly against the wall box, using your hand. The imprint of the wall box will be transferred to the back of the panel, exactly where the cut should be made.

- If you measure for cut-outs, use the same-size wall or junction box as a template for marking the cut. This helps avoid incorrect measurements. Drill holes in the corners of the cut-out, keeping within the lines to avoid over-cutting. Use a sabre saw or a keyhole saw to cut out the opening. The hole may be cut slightly larger than the box since the face plate will cover the area.

- For window openings, measure from the edge of the last installed panel to the edge of the opening and from the floor to the opening, allowing for the space you are leaving between the floor and panel bottom (¼–½ inch).
- Place a panel face down on your work benches (if using a power saw) and transfer the opening's measurements. Make the cut.
- Wire brush all stud nailing surfaces when using adhesives to install panels directly to the studs. This ensures a good bond.
- Apply adhesives with a regular caulking gun. Cut the applicator to dispense a ⅛-inch bead. Apply a continuous bead of adhesive at panel joints, and at the top and bottom plates. Place 3-inch-long beads 6 inches apart on intermediate studs.
- Now put the panel in place, keeping the gap between panel and floor. Tack panel at top with color-matching nails. Check to be sure the panel is where you want it. Push the panel on the adhesive with firm, uniform pressure to spread the adhesive beads evenly between panel and framing members.
- Now grasp the bottom of the panel and slowly pull the panel out and away from the framing. Allow the time specified by the adhesive manufacturer to pass, then press the panel firmly against the framing. Go over all intermediate stud areas and edges, applying pressure to get a firm bond and even panel surface.
- For door openings, use the same procedure you followed for window openings. Lay out the opening's measurements on the panel and cut it out. Always double-check your measurements and their position on the panel.

The most logical installation procedure is to start at one corner and work around the room. You will want to install panels with random-width planks the same way; i.e., if the first panel is installed with the narrow plank on the left side, then all panels should be installed with the narrow plank on the left side.

Whether your project calls for painted, papered, or vinyl-covered wallboard, wood or hardboard paneling, to begin right is to finish right. Your new wall can look completely professional. Trim work will be covered in Chapter 4.

HOW TO DETERMINE MATERIALS NEEDED

Estimate drywall, plywood, and hardboard panel requirements by room size. Multiply the wall length by the wall height to get number of square feet. When installing drywall, deduct the square feet of door and window openings. For best results, door and window openings should be cut out of wood panels to maintain panel continuity, so do not deduct for standard openings.

Multiply ceiling length by ceiling width for total square footage and divide by the square footage of the panel size used in the ceiling. Here's an example:

Room size   12' × 14'
Ceiling square feet   168
Panels needed   Six 4 × 8 panels = 192 SF
                       or
                       Four, 4 × 12 panels = 192 SF

Figure 3-14 describes how to determine the amount of drywall required for the walls of a room.

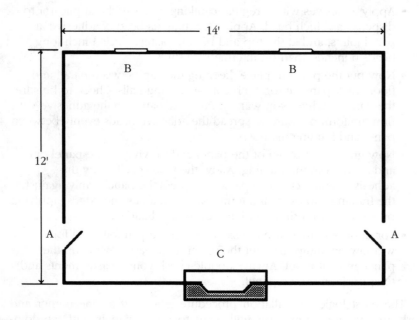

Determine the perimeter of walls: 12' × 14' = 12' + 12' + 14' + 14' = 52' or 13 panels. For drywall allow for windows, doors, and fireplace openings, etc. Use the following deductions:

Door   1/2 panel   A
Window   1/4 panel   B
Fireplace   1/2 panel   C

Based on a ceiling height of 8 feet or less, the actual number of panels for the room would be 11 pieces.

3-14 Determining number of drywall panels needed.

Other Materials

When hanging drywall; in addition to the paneling you will need:

1   5 gallon can joint compound (per 1,000 square feet of wallboard) for texture-finished ceilings using joint compound, allow 5 gallons per 400 square feet.

5¼ lb.   1⅜" annular ring nails (per 1,000 square feet of wallboard).

1   250' of tape (per 600 square feet of wallboard)

1   8' metal corner bead (per each 8 foot outside corner.)

HOW TO COMPUTE YOUR LABOR HOURS

It is pretty well established how much time professionals need to do a specific job. For example, a crew consisting of one hanger and one laborer can install 100 square feet of ⅜-inch-thick drywall to stud framing in 1.8 hours. For ceiling work, add 0.6 hours for a total of 2.4 hours. Time includes hanging, taping, joint finishing and sanding. For ½-inch-thick sheet rock, figure 1.9 hours per 100 square feet for wall application.

One hundred square feet of 4 × 8 panels is 3.125 sheets. Thus, the professional might complete the walls of a 14 × 16 room in 5 hours, or 20 minutes per panel; the 224 square feet ceiling in about 3½ hours, or 30 minutes per panel. If you have never worked with drywall it will take you much longer to install it. Learners should take all the time they need to do the job right. If you have some experience hanging and finishing drywall, allow at least 90 minutes per ceiling panel and 60 minutes per wall panel.

The professional can install and trim out a 14 × 16 room with ¼-inch-thick wood panels in approximately 16 hours, or about 65 minutes for each panel. Allow yourself at least twice that time.

Chapter 4

Ceilings

Ceiling height is generally mandated by code, and your ceiling must comply with those regulations.

Check your basement ceiling height. A basement without habitable space can be as low as 6'8" (6'4" under girders). Basement with habitable space require a ceiling height of 7'6". If you install a luminous or drop ceiling, locate it so you will have a minimum finished ceiling height of 7'0".

Most codes will not permit the ceiling to be dropped below 7'6". In attic rooms with a sloping ceiling, at least half of the room must have the ceiling at least 7'6" high. Where exposed beams or girders are spaced at least 48 inches on center, the bottom of the beam or girder should be at least 7 feet from the floor. Generally, you will want to partition off (with knee walls) any portion of floor area having less than a 5 foot ceiling height (see FIG. 4-1). The building code in your area will probably specify a minimum ceiling height of 6'8" for halls, bathrooms, and utility rooms.

A ceiling can be of any texture and design you imagine it to be. It can be of covered wallboard, to mirrors, to plank and beam (FIG. 4-2). A ceiling can be flat or it can follow the contours of the rafters in a cathedral style ceiling.

The finish ceiling must attach to something solid that is intelligently laid out to accommodate the various-size ceiling materials, while maintaining structural strength. If you are going to redo a ceiling, such as lowering it or replacing the existing finish, you need to know what constitutes a ceiling and how the framing can affect your project.

Most one-story houses will have 2 × 6 ceiling joists spaced 16 or 24 inches o.c. Since the ceiling joists of two-story houses are also the floor joists for the story above, the joists may be of any size from 2 × 8s to 2 × 12s, spaced 12, 16, 20, or 24 inches o.c.

Most houses have a load-bearing partition near the center of the structure. The ceiling joists either rest on it or join on it. Ceiling joists seldom span the entire width of the building as trusses do. Ceiling joists in most gable roof framing run straight from side wall to side wall. In a hip roof the run of the regular joists stops short of the outside wall to allow clearance for the hip and jack rafters. Short ceiling joists are installed perpen-

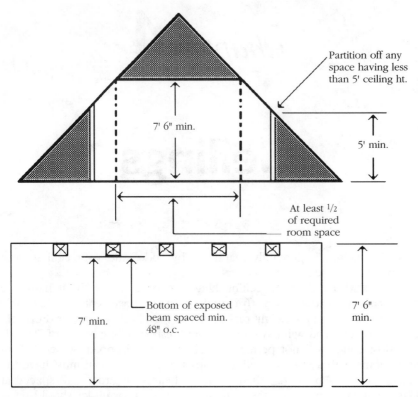

Partition off any
space having less
than 5' ceiling ht.

7' 6" min.

5' min.

At least ½
of required
room space

Bottom of exposed
beam spaced min.
48" o.c.

7' min.

7' 6"
min.

4-1 Required ceiling heights.

Merillat Industries, Inc.

4-2 Kitchen ceiling with exposed beams.

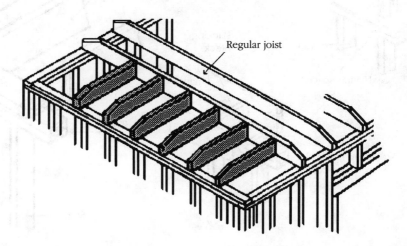

Short joist

Regular joist

4-3 Ceiling joist layout for hip rafters of hip roof.

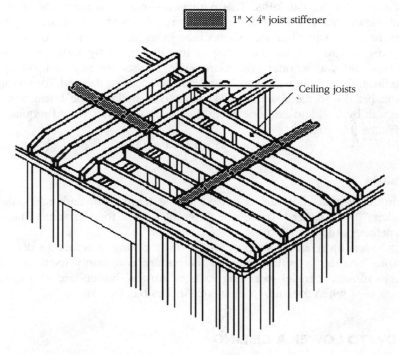

1" × 4" joist stiffener

Ceiling joists

4-4 Installing ceiling joists in two directions.

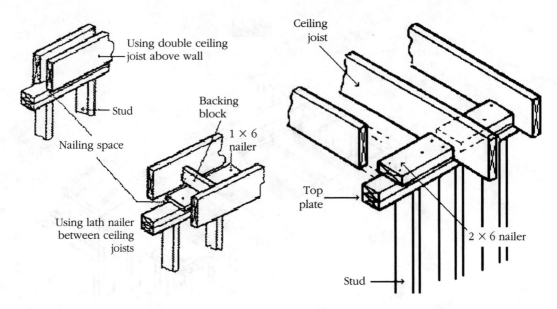

4-5 Lath nailers at wall/ceiling juncture.

dicular to the regular joists. This permits the rafters to reach the outside wall plates (FIG. 4-3). It is not an absolute requirement that all ceiling joists run the same way. Figure 4-4 shows how joists may run in two directions.

If you plan to lower the ceiling in that old house by adding a second ceiling, and you wonder how many ceiling joists are required, multiply the linear feet of the wall by 0.75 and add one joist to the end, for spacing 16 inches o.c. If the spacing is 24 inches o.c., multiply the linear feet of the wall by 0.50 and add one joist. Thus, a 16-foot wall would require 13 joists for 16" spacing:

$$16 \times 0.75 = 12 + 1 = 13$$

Nailers

Many do-it-yourselfers are confused by the terms "lath nailers," "ceiling nailers," and "nailer." These are different names for the same thing— something solid to nail to.

Nailers form nailing support for the finish ceiling, whether it's drywall, furring boards, or ceiling panels. Nailers are commonly used on wall plates running parallel to ceiling joists or trusses. Nailers are also sometimes used when the joist spacing is 24 inches o.c. (see FIG. 4-5).

HOW TO LOWER A CEILING

Adding a true ceiling at a lower height entails installing new ceiling joist members. A drop, or suspended, ceiling is composed of a grid-work of metal main runners and cross tees. The new ceiling can be finished using drywall, ceiling tile, hardboard, etc. Insulation may be added to the ceiling.

Depending on the span, spacing, and method of installation, new joist members may be 2 × 4s or larger. There are three basic ways to install wood ceiling joists in your lowered ceiling. You can tie in:

1. With cripple stud support.

2. To joist header.

3. Using joist hangers.

Figure 4-6 shows how to add ceiling joists. If you have access to the wall frame (no finish wall installed), you can nail a cripple to a stud to support the joist, as seen in FIG. 4-7. The alternative method is to nail a

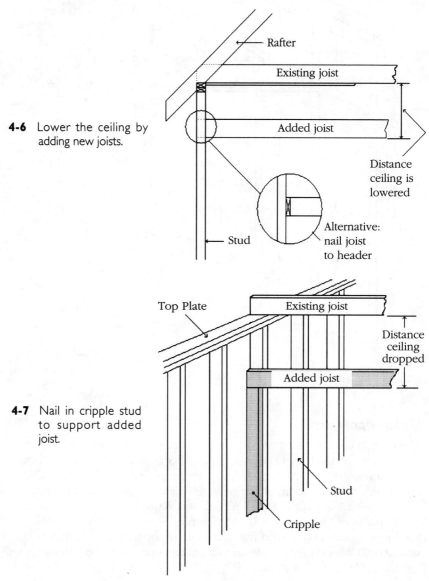

4-6 Lower the ceiling by adding new joists.

4-7 Nail in cripple stud to support added joist.

joist header the same size as the joist to the studs to support the added joists, depicted in FIG. 4-8. Your new ceiling can be a cathedral ceiling, illustrated in FIG. 4-9. Face-nail the added joist to the existing joists at ceiling's peak using three 16d nails. Or, use 1 × 4 boards as joist hangers, as shown in FIG. 4-10. Let's take a look at each procedure.

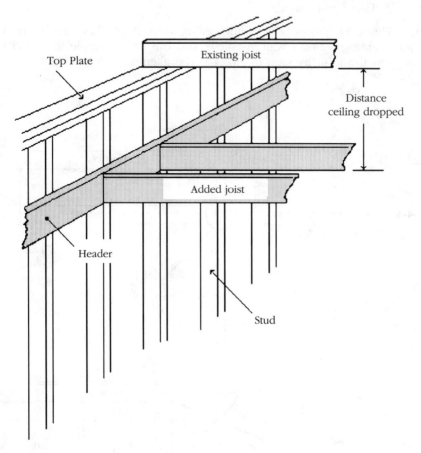

4-8 Nail header to studs and added joists to header.

Using cripple studs

The cripple (or jack stud) provides maximum support for the joist member and ceiling finish. It can support large joists over a long span. Access to the wall framing is necessary. Measure the cripple to rest on the sole plate and extend to the bottom of the new ceiling joists. Face-nail the cripple to the stud with 10d nails space 16 inches and staggered.

Rest the end of the joists on the cripple, as shown in FIG. 4-7. Face-nail the joists to the stud with three 12d nails. Prior to installing the cripples you should check the floor level. To make certain your new ceiling will

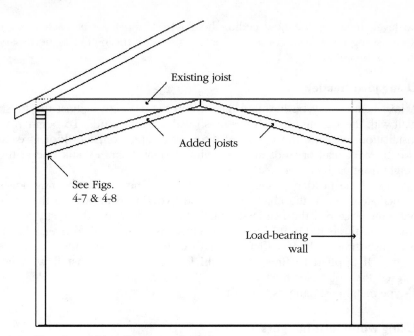

4-9 Changing a high ceiling to a cathedral type.

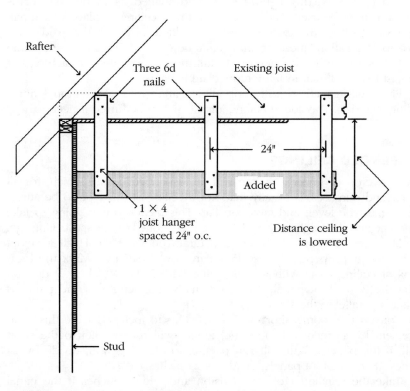

4-10 Tie added joist to existing joist with 1 × 4 hangers.

be level, measure the new ceiling height from the floor at each corner. Run a string level from corner to corner, adjusting the height as necessary to level the ceiling.

Using joist header

A joist header may be installed directly on the studs or against the finish wall with the nailing through the finish wall into the studs. To begin your installation, measure the height of the new ceiling from the floor at each corner. Mark wall or studs at new ceiling height. Snap a chalk line at the height from each corner.

Install the header, placing a member the same size as the new joists immediately above the chalk line on the two side walls where the joists will butt. Face-nail the header to each stud. When applied directly to the studs, use three 10d or 12d nails at each stud. When applied over a finish wall, use three nails of sufficient length to penetrate the studs at least 1½ inches. If applied to finish walls thicker than ¾ inch, install with lag screws. Pre-drill holes for the screws. Secure the joists to the header with U-type metal joist hangers (FIG. 4-10).

Using wood joist hangers

You can suspend the added ceiling joists with 1 × 4 wood members secured to the existing ceiling joists and spaced 24 inches o.c. (This method cannot be used where there is a finish ceiling in place.) Face-nail the 1 × 4s to both the existing joist and added joist with three 6d nails. Prior to installation, measure and mark new ceiling height in the same manner as for the header method. Install the 1 × 4 hangers at each end of the joist first, and then install intermediate hangers.

Either tie-in method will support insulation and conventional finish ceiling materials. The added ceiling joists can also be furred if necessary.

SUSPENDED CEILINGS

You can drop or lower a ceiling with a suspended ceiling which, for all intents and purposes, is exactly that. For a ceiling of this type to be attractive, it must be level, and table-top flat. This means you're going to take your time and do it right. If you don't, you have one big mess as ceilings go.

Measure the room and draw a diagram on what we'll call a layout sheet; use graph paper at least 45 squares by 29 squares. Mark the locations of ceiling joists with a dotted line (FIG. 4-11). Which way do you want the 2 × 4 foot panels to run? Usually, the length of the panel is installed parallel to the short wall.

Convert the room's short-wall dimensions to inches. Divide this measurement by 48 inches if the panel length will run parallel to the short wall. If the panel length will run parallel to the long wall, divide by 24 inches. (For 2 × 2-foot panels, divide by 24 inches.)

Take the remainder of this division and add 48 inches if the panel length will run parallel to the short wall. Add 24 inches if the panel length

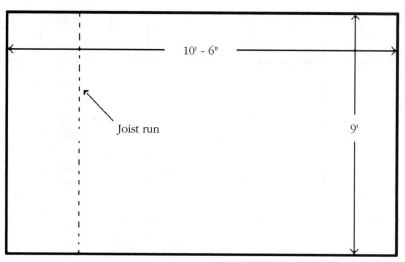

4-11 Mark ceiling joist run and indicate ceiling size.

will run parallel to the long wall. (For 2 × 2-foot panels, add 24 inches.) Round off to the nearest whole number. Half this figure equals the border dimensions at each side of the room.

Let's look at an example. For a room 13 feet wide with the panel length running parallel to the short wall:

1. Convert 13 feet to 156 inches.
2. Divide 156 by 48 equals 3.25 or 3 panel lengths with a remainder of 12 inches.
3. The remaining 12 inches plus 48 inches equal 60 inches.
4. Divide 60 by 2, which equals 30 inches.

Thus, the border panels at each side will be 30 inches. The number of full panels running across the room will be two. This dimension (30 inches) also equals the distance of the first main runner from the sidewalls. Find the end border panel size by repeating the above steps for the length of the room.

Your next step is to draw the gridwork pattern of your layout (FIG. 4-12 shows how it should look). Draw the first and last main runners at the border tile distance from the sidewalls, and perpendicular (90-degree angle) to the ceiling joists. Draw the interior main runners at 4-foot intervals. Use a different-color pencil to mark the cross tees—start with the border tile distance from the end walls, then add the interior cross tees at 2-foot intervals. The cross tees will intersect with the main runners.

Hold on to your layout sheet. You'll need it to figure the number of grid components and material needed for the suspended ceiling.

Wall molding

Determine the exact position for the new suspended ceiling, keeping in mind you need at least 3½ inches of space below the existing ceiling or

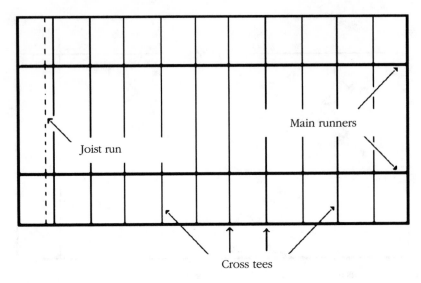

Joist run

Main runners

Cross tees

4-12 How to lay out main runners and cross tees.

exposed joists. Allow space (6 inches between fixture and ceiling) for any light fixtures that will be located above the ceiling.

Draw a level line completely around the room at the new ceiling height. Use a level: you want accuracy. Don't assume the existing ceiling is level if you measured the new ceiling height from that point. Don't assume the floor is level if you measured from that point, whether you're working in the basement, attic, or on the main floor. If you're doing the basement, set the ceiling as low as possible to cover ducts, pipes, etc. When you are satisfied that your measurements are level, snap a chalk line on each wall.

Wall molding, or angle (FIG. 4-13), is available in 10-foot lengths. Measure the room's perimeter, and divide by 10 to find the number of wall molding sections needed for the job.

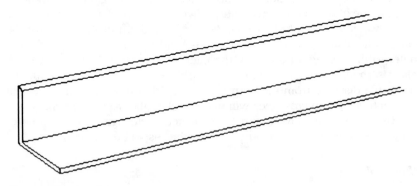

4-13 Wall molding.

Attach the wall molding to the wall all around the room, placing the flange at the level line (FIG. 4-14). Nail firmly to studs. Use screw anchors or other masonry fasteners to attach molding to brick or masonry walls. Treat the corners as shown in FIG. 4-15; use a hacksaw or snips to cut angles.

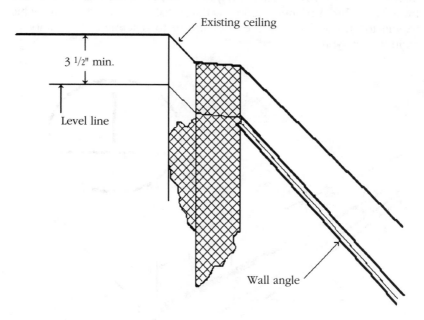

4-14 Install wall angle at level line.

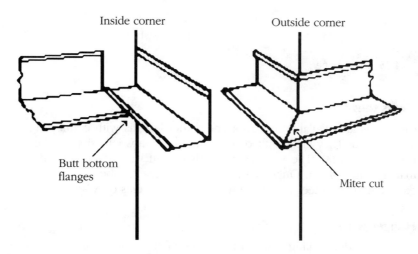

4-15 Wall angle corner treatment.

Main runners

Main runners, or main tees, (FIG. 4-16) are available in 12 foot lengths and have cross tee slots every 12 inches, beginning 6 inches from each end. Tabs at each end make it possible to join main runners for lengths longer than 12 feet (FIG. 4-17). You cannot, however, cut more than two sections from each 12 foot runner: a third section would have no tabs with which to join to another runner. Use your layout to determine the number of main runners you need.

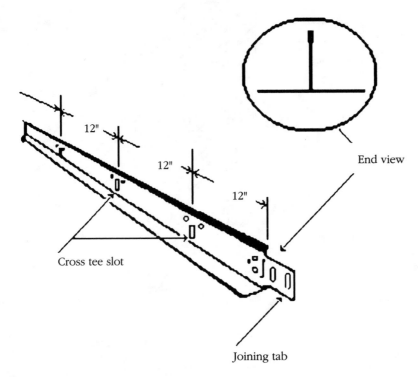

End view

12"

12"

12"

Cross tee slot

Joining tab

4-16 Main runner.

Cross tees

Cross tees are available in 2 foot and 4 foot lengths with connecting tabs at each end. They are installed by inserting the tabs into slots in the main runner (FIG. 4-18). The way to attach them will vary, depending on who manufactured them. Only two border cross tees can be cut from a standard-length cross tee. Count the number of cross tees on your layout.

Hanger wire

The suspended ceiling gridwork consists of the main runners and cross tees. The gridwork is suspended with wire from structural members such

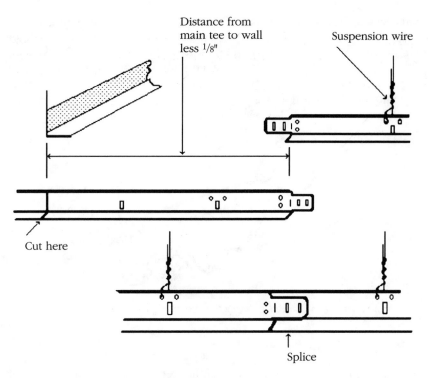

Distance from
main tee to wall
less $1/8"$

Suspension wire

Cut here

Splice

4-17 Measure, cut, and splice for rooms wider than 12 feet.

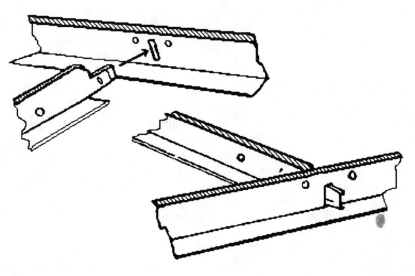

4-18 Joining cross tee to main runner.

as the ceiling joists. The main runners are suspended with hanger wire every 4 feet. Make the wire at each suspension point 6–8 inches longer than the distance between the joist and new ceiling. Use 16-gauge wire.

Use wire fasteners (FIG. 4-19) at each support point to attach wire to the joist. Install the fasteners every 4 feet and on each side of every main runner joint.

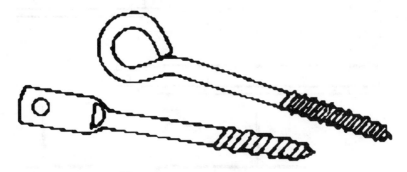

4-19 Use strong wire fasteners to anchor the ceiling to joists.

Ceiling panels

Count the number of ceiling panels indicated on your layout. Allow for cutting border panels. Remember that the panel is designed to support only itself—do not try to use the suspended ceiling to support insulation.

Lighting panels

Lighting, or translucent plastic, panels are used in conjunction with lighting fixtures installed above the suspended ceiling. A two-tube fluorescent fixture centered over a 2 × 4-foot luminous panel makes an attractive light arrangement for your new ceiling.

INSTALLATION STEPS

Before beginning to install your suspended ceiling, remove ceiling panels from the package 24 hours prior to installation to allow the panels to adjust to the normal conditions of the site.

The first step is to measure the new ceiling height in each corner of the room, allowing a minimum of 3½ inches below the level of the existing ceiling or exposed joists. Don't forget to allow a minimum of 6 inches between light fixtures and the new ceiling.

Snap a chalk line through the measurement marks on each wall. Now is the time to check the level of the chalk lines. Use a 4-foot level if you have one. Adjust the chalk lines to ensure a level ceiling. Then secure the wall molding along the chalk lines, treating corners as in FIG. 4-15.

The next step is to install main runners. Refer to your layout, and locate the position of the first main runner. At this location, snap a chalk line on the old ceiling or joists. Continue marking the position of all main runners, snapping a chalk line every 4 feet, parallel to the first main runner line. Install screw-eye fasteners to the joist every 4 feet where the ceiling joists intersect with the main runner chalk line. Attach hanger wire to each screw eye, securely wrapping the wire around itself at least three times. Make sure the hanger wire is at least 6–8 inches longer than the distance between the old ceiling and main runner.

In the next step, unless cross tees for border tiles fall exactly on a main runner cross tee slot (see FIG. 4-16), you must cut the main runner to fit. Select a corner to start your installation. At the border-panel distance from each wall, stretch two reference strings, each at a 90-degree angle to the other. Secure the strings to the wall immediately below the wall molding. These reference strings will serve as a guide for cutting main runners and cross tees (refer to FIG. 4-20).

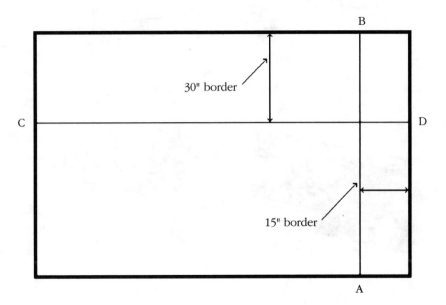

4-20 Layout for border tile.

Using reference string AB as a guide, measure each main runner individually. (Do not use the first main runner as a pattern for cutting.) Cut the main runner so the first reference string falls on a cross tee slot (FIG. 4-21). Locate the wire-support hole (a small, round hole at the top of the main runner) farthest from the starting end wall and closest to the last hanger wire. Mark the hole on the first main runner (FIG. 4-22).

Now carry the main runner to a side wall and lay it on the wall molding with the cut end butting against the end wall. Mark the sidewall through the main runner and drive a nail into the wall at the point marked.

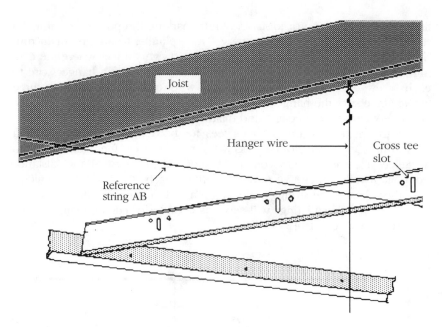

4-21 Use reference string to determine placement of main runner.

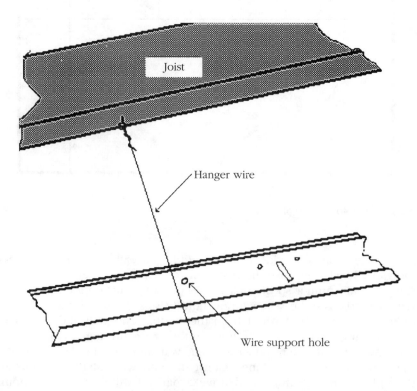

4-22 Locate and mark wire support hole in main runner.

Repeat this last step on the opposite side of the room. Stretch a string from nail to nail and align each hanger wire so it intersects with the string. Make a 90-degree bend in hanger wires where they meet the string.

Then rest the cut end of the first main runner on the end-wall molding. Run the pre bent hanger wire through the support hole. Secure it by bending it up and twisting the wire around itself at least three times. Align the rest of the hanger wires to the nearest support holes, making a 90-degree bend where they intersect the top of the support holes. Twist the wire three times to secure it.

For long rooms, connect as many main-runner sections as needed to reach the other end of the room. Cut the excess main runner with snips and use this piece to start the next row. Repeat this same procedure for the remaining rows, bending and attaching hanger wire as before.

Always cut each main runner so a cross tee slot aligns with reference string AB. Install a hanger wire close to the point where two main runners are connected. Install an additional hanger wire if necessary. Check the level of each main runner (FIG. 4-23).

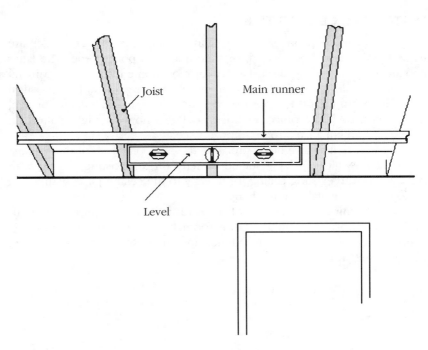

4-23 Use a level to ascertain that main runners are properly positioned.

Next step: begin by placing the full 4-foot cross tees in rows away from the borders. When in place, lay in a few full ceiling panels to help stabilize and square the entire grid system.

Cut the first row of cross tees for the border tile, measuring each individually and using reference string CD as a guide. When you measure each cross tee, align the edge of the first main runner with the reference string under it. Measure from the side wall to the near edge of the main runner.

Cut the cross tee to this dimension and install. Continue in this manner, cutting each cross tee individually along the first wall. Follow the same procedure to cut tees for the last row along the opposite border. Then attach the 4-foot cross tees to main runners across the room at 2-foot intervals and lock them in. If you're using 2 x 2-foot panels, attach cross tees at the mid-points of the 4-foot cross tees.

You can then measure and cut border panels individually. A cross tee or a section of a main runner can be used as a straight edge. Cut panels face up with a sharp utility knife. To drop panels into position, tilt slightly, lift above the framework, and rest the edge on the cross tee and main runner. Drop into place.

You can cut translucent plastic lighting panels by scoring them repeatedly with a sharp knife until the panel is cut through. Install the panel with the glossy side (or smooth side) up.

INSTALLING CEILING TILE

Ceiling tile can be plain or have elegantly sculptured designs. Tiles are made from mineral fiber, wood, or cane fiber and polystyrene. The latter two are lower in cost, and satisfactory for most home installations. Mineral fiber tiles should be used where high fire ratings are applicable. Acoustical tiles can absorb the greater portion of a room's noise and is ideal for den, game room, or home office. Figure 4-24 shows how the right pattern in ceiling tile can enhance a room's appearance.

The 12 x 12-inch size tile is probably the most practical for the average room. Ceiling tile can be installed directly on an existing ceiling with cement, over an existing ceiling, or directly to the ceiling joists with wood furring strips or metal channel hangers.

To determine the number of 12 x 12-inch tiles required for your project, multiply the length of the room by the width, and add one extra tile, or 12 inches, to each dimension to allow for cuts and fitting. Let's do an example:

Room length	18'+1' =19'
Room width	14'+1' =15'
	(19' x 15'=285)
Total tiles need	285

If the room doesn't measure an exact number of feet, use the next highest number. Thus, a room 17 feet 5 inches x 12 feet 7 inches would be treated as 18 feet x 13 feet, and one tile would be added to each dimension (19 x 14=266 tiles required).

The room must have a ceiling balanced in appearance and in fact. You cannot start with a full tile at a border and hope for luck to bring you out even in the end. The border tiles on opposite sides of the room

Quaker Maid.

4-24 You can select a ceiling tile for its appearance as well as noise absorption.

should be the same width, and the width should be more than one-half the width of a 12-inch tile.

To determine how wide a border tile should be, measure the short wall of the room first. If the wall does not measure an exact number of feet, simply add 12 inches to the odd inches left over, and complete the calculations as shown in FIG. 4-25.

If your redesign project involves removing a partition, the old ceiling might need covering. If there is an existing ceiling in your basement conver-

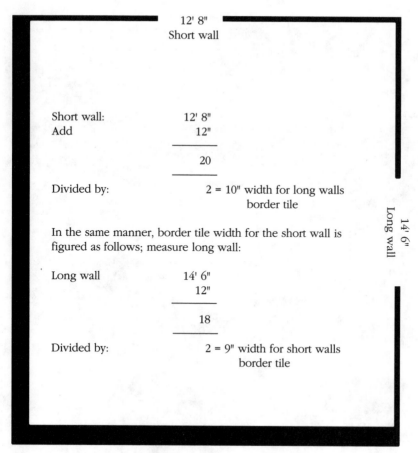

12' 8"
Short wall

Short wall: 12' 8"
Add   12"
_____

20
_____

Divided by: 2 = 10" width for long walls
border tile

In the same manner, border tile width for the short wall is figured as follows; measure long wall:

Long wall   14' 6"
                    12"
_____

18
_____

Divided by: 2 = 9" width for short walls
border tile

14' 6"
Long wall

4-25 Establishing the size of the border tiles.

sion, it might need re-doing. You cannot cement ceiling tile to just any surface. A sound, level ceiling is required. Remove old wallpaper, flaking, etc.

Measure the room to ensure that border tiles will be the same width on opposite sides (see FIG. 4-26). For your next step, snap a chalk line to align the first row of border tiles along the long and short walls (FIG. 4-27). For this discussion, we assume the room is square. Out-of-square rooms can be a problem and are dealt with later.

Now cut (face up) the first border tile to size with a sharp utility knife. This tile will fit into a corner, so you have the two measurements of the end wall (short) and the side wall (long) to consider. Thus, if your border tiles on the long side of the room are 9 inches, and 7 inches on the short side, the corner border tile must be cut twice to make it 9 × 7 so all other border tiles on both the long and short walls will line up with it properly.

Place 5 thin daubs of cement on the first border tile—a dab at each corner and one in the center. Be sure to follow the instructions on the can. Staple each flange to hold the tile in position while the cement dries.

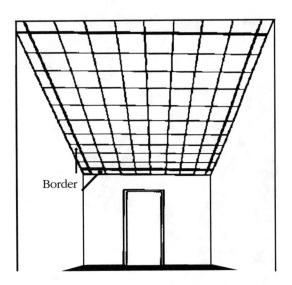

4-26 Border tiles on opposite sides of room should be of same width.

Border

4-27 Lay out border tile with a chalk line.

Chalk lines

Border tile width

If you have carefully examined the ceiling tile you will notice that the tile can only be installed with the stapling flange lined up on the chalk line and the flange exposed so the tongue of the next tile can slide into place, ensuring a neat and firm fit (FIG. 4-28).

Note the position and run of tongue and flange. If installation is a checkerboard pattern, separate the tile into two stacks according to the grain/tongue and flange run. To avoid contraction and expansion problems, store the tile in the room 24 hours before installation.

Work across the ceiling, installing two or three border tiles at a time. Fill-in between the border tiles with full-size tiles (FIG. 4-29). When you have worked your way to the opposite wall, measure and cut each tile to fit. Once all the tiles are in place, install molding to finish the ceiling.

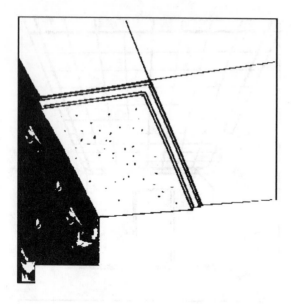

4-28 Line up the stapling flange on the chalk line.

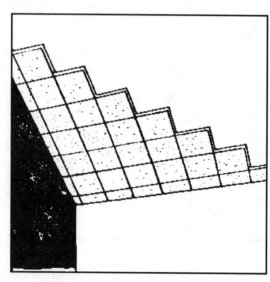

4-29 Installing tiles across ceiling.

While you are installing furring strips (or using the cement method) to install tiles, suppose you discover the room is not square. How will that affect the appearance of the ceiling? The results will be terrible. You have to do something to correct the problem.

Nail wood furring strips to the ceiling joists at right angles to the joists. Use seasoned 1-x-3 or 1-x-4 softwood boards. When installing furring strips over an existing ceiling, first locate and mark (with a chalk line) each joist run. Nail furring to each joist using two nails of sufficient length to penetrate the joist a minimum of 1½ inch.

Install the first furring strip immediately against the wall that runs perpendicular to the ceiling joists. Nail up the second furring strip, locating the center of the second strip the same distance from the wall as the width of the border tile. Carefully install the remaining furring strips parallel to the second furring strip, 12 inches o.c. (the ceiling tile width). To maintain accuracy, cut a piece of furring strip 12 inches, less the width of one furring strip, and use this as a guide in spacing the third and remaining strips. The block is used as a spacer between the strips as you hold the strip in position while nailing.

Unless the ceiling joists are all level on the same plane (they seldom are) the furring strips must be adjusted at the offending joists.

After locating and marking with a chalk line the position of each furring strip, stretch a string under the bottom of the ceiling joists to identify high and low spots. Shave or shim the joists as necessary. At the walls running at right angles to the furring strips, you can use blocks of furring between the strips to provide a nailer for the border tiles.

MEASURING AND MARKING TILE LAYOUT

Keep in mind that we are working with a ceiling that is out-of-square. After the furring strips are installed, begin by snapping the first chalk line on the wood furring strip (or if you're using the cement method, on the existing ceiling), parallel to the starting side wall.

Let's take an example: the side wall border is 10 inches. Adding ½ inch for the stapling flange, the first chalk line will be 10½ inches from the side wall (FIG. 4-30).

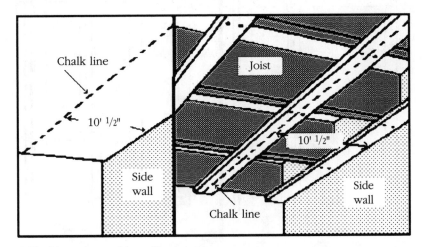

4-30 Measuring position of furring strips.

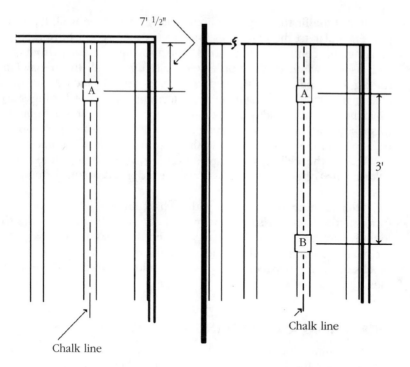

4-31 Beginning tile layout for off-square ceiling.

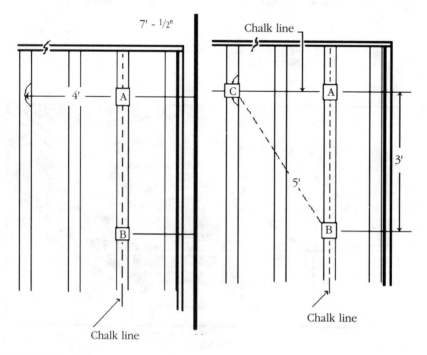

4-32 Striking first and second arc.

The second chalk line must be at a right angle to the first chalk line or the tiles won't line up properly. To ensure a perfect right angle, do this: Measure the width of the end wall border tile (7 inches) plus ½ inch, and mark point A on your first chalk line, as shown in FIG. 4-31. Next, measure exactly 3 feet from point A, and mark point B. Now measure exactly 4 feet from point A and strike an arc (FIG 4-32). From point B, measure exactly 5 feet toward the first arc, and strike a second arc.

Look closely at the point where the two arcs intersect. Mark this point C. Snap the second chalk line through points A and C. Check the squareness of the two chalk lines with a carpenter's square. These steps allow the wall side of the border tiles to take up the difference caused by the *un*-square ceiling. Therefore, measure for each border tile, as the measurements will be different.

Now measure the first border tile (FIG. 4-33). Cut the tile using a carpenter's square and a sharp utility knife. Fit the border tile in position in the corner of the room. Line the stapling flange up with the chalk line, and staple. Keep the pattern even. Work across the ceiling as shown in FIG. 4-29.

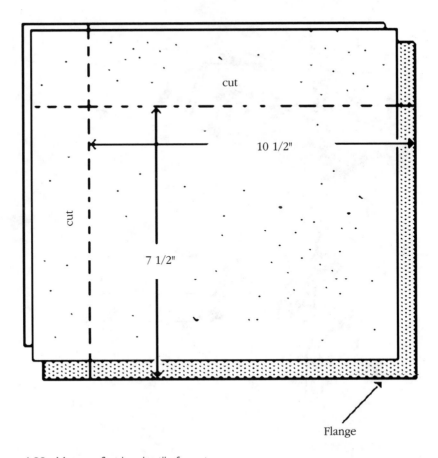

cut

10 1/2"

cut

7 1/2"

Flange

4-33 Measure first border tile for cut.

TRIM WORK

Don't feel bad about not looking forward to trimming out your project—if that is the case. Many professional carpenters steer away from fitting trim whenever possible. With a little patience, however, the trim-out should proceed with a minimum of flaws.

Moldings are strips of wood ripped from kiln-dried boards up to 16 feet long. There are about 30 different stock patterns, or profiles. Each profile is designed for a specific purpose, and most have secondary uses as well. Some do-it-yourselfers are able to design and make their own molding, using a table saw with molding cutter-bit sets. Figure 4-34 shows how to miter, splice, and cope cove molding.

Mitering Most molding joints are cut on a 45-degree angle, as shown in A, FIG. 4-34. Set your miter box at 45 degrees, and trim (at opposite angles) each of the two pieces to be mated. When mitering cove molding for corner fits, place the molding in the miter box so it is upside down and end-reversed to the way it will be installed.

Splicing When splicing two lengths of molding, as shown in B, FIG. 4-34, place the molding flat on its back in the miter box. Miter at identical

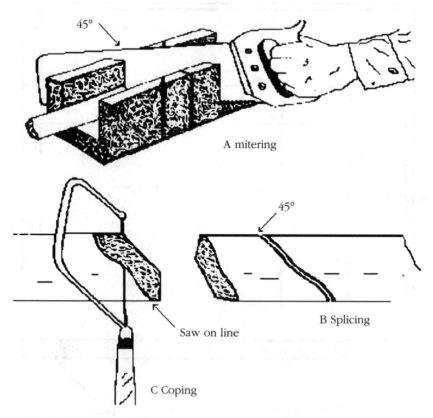

45°

A mitering

45°

B Splicing

Saw on line

C Coping

4-34 Cutting molding to fit.

45-degree angles the ends to be joined. Butt the ends together for a smooth fit.

Coping Place the molding in the miter box and position it upright against the back plate. Make a 45-degree cut. The cut exposes the profile of the molding. With the profile serving as a template, cut along the profile edge with a coping saw. Trim away a wedge at another 45-degree angle. This duplicates the pattern so it fits over the face of the adjoining molding. This will require a bit of practice for most do-it-yourselfers. Figure 4-35 shows how to install base molding pieces. Calculate your trim requirements from the room size and add 10 percent for waste and end cutting.

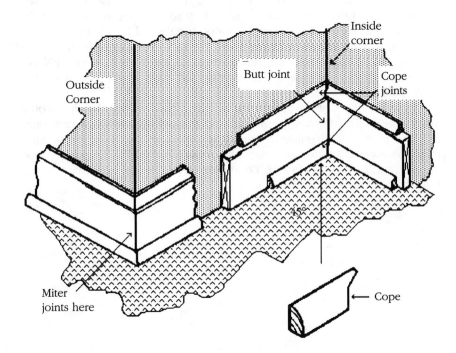

4-35 Cuts and fits for base molding.

Finishes Paint, lacquer, enamel, shellac, stain, or varnish can be used on unfinished softwood molding. Fill nail holes with wood putty and sand the wood to a smooth, clean surface with #00 or finer sandpaper. Sand with the grain. Apply a primer if you use paint or enamel. Prefinished vinyl moldings are available in many wood-grain color tones.

HOW TO COMPUTE YOUR LABOR HOURS

A skilled carpenter can install 65 board feet of 2-x-6 ceiling joist in conventional framing in one hour. A 2-x-6 twelve feet in length contains 12 board feet. Our carpenter thus installs 5.41 ceiling joists in one hour. A room 16 × 12 requires 13 joists space 16 inches o.c., for a total of 156 board feet, and will take the carpenter about 2½ hours. Add another 2 hours to measure for and install the joist headers or the cripple studs.

The first time do-it-yourselfer with average skills should triple the professional's time, taking about 13½ hours. Installing the joist with wood joist hangers will require about 24 hours.

The first time do-it-yourselfer should be able to install a suspended ceiling at the rate of 50 square feet per 8 hours. Thus, a 16 × 12 ceiling (192 square feet) would require about 30 hours. (A professional could do the same ceiling in about 8 hours.)

The first time do-it-yourselfer should be able to install adhesive-mounted 12-x–12 ceiling tile at the rate of 50 square feet in 4 hours. A 16 × 12 ceiling would require about 15 hours. Installing 12-x-12 ceiling tile to furring strips with staples will take about the same number of hours.

The time it takes to install furring strips depends on how much shaving and shimming is required. The average job takes about 30 minutes for each 12-foot strip.

Hour estimates should never be a major concern for the do-it-yourselfer. The hour estimates given here and throughout the book can, only at best, be a general guide to help you get some idea how much time might be involved: how much commitment is required for the project. The important thing is to get the job done right, regardless of how many hours it might take.

Chapter **5**

Floors

Basement floors are commonly concrete slabs below grade. A basement floor slab is poured on a gravel base and supported by a well-drained footing. A vapor barrier is placed between the gravel base and the slab. You cannot see these details in a finished basement.

Attic floors come in many different configurations. The attic floor framing is the ceiling framing of the rooms below, and may be any size members, from 2 × 4 to 2 × 8 or larger. Most ceilings are framed with 2 × 6 members spaced 16 inches or 24 inches on center. Therefore, unless the attic was designed to be later finished as habitable space and provided with adequate-size floor joists, you will have to reinforce the floor joists. If the attic is floored you may have to remove a section to determine joist size and spacing.

ALLOWABLE SPAN

If your attic has a structurally sound floor, such as 2 × 8s spaced 16 inches on center over a span not exceeding 12 feet, you are in luck; the framing falls in the allowable span range. The term "allowable span" for lumber joists refers to the clear span between supports. The three things that determine what the clear span of joist should be are:

- The working stress for the joist grade and species.
- The joist size and spacing.
- The design load specified in the building code.

Most standards limit joist deflection to $\frac{1}{360}$ of the span under a 40-pound per square foot (or smaller) uniform live load. The joists must be strong enough to carry the live load (contents of the room) plus a dead load (the building itself) of 10 pounds per square foot.

Your building supply house can furnish you with the span limitation on most lumber species and sizes. Keep in mind that lumber sizes are not what they purport to be. A 2 × 8 is not really a 2 × 8; it is only 1½ inches thick by 7¼ inches wide. Lumber is identified and sold by the nominal size—the size before it is planed, or dressed. A green size is also a category that can complicate matters when you are trying to get a perfect fit. TABLE 5-1 is the nominal size chart for some softwood lumber. Use the table when you're trying to fit the pieces together in a set dimension. A green size will change when the lumber cures, becoming the actual size.

Table 5-1 Nominal size chart for softwood lumber.

Nominal Size	*Green Size*	*Dry Size*
1 × 4	$\frac{25}{32} \times 3\frac{9}{16}$	¾ × 3½
1 × 6	$\frac{25}{32} \times 5\frac{5}{8}$	¾ × 5½
2 × 4	$1\frac{9}{16} \times 3\frac{9}{16}$	1½ × 3½
2 × 6	$1\frac{9}{16} \times 5\frac{5}{8}$	1½ × 5½
2 × 8	$1\frac{9}{16} \times 7\frac{1}{2}$	1½ × 7¼
2 × 10	$1\frac{9}{16} \times 9\frac{1}{2}$	1½ × 9¼
2 × 12	$1\frac{9}{16} \times 11\frac{1}{2}$	1½ × 11¼
4 × 4	$3\frac{9}{16} \times 3\frac{9}{16}$	3½ × 3/2
4 × 6	$3\frac{9}{16} \times 5\frac{5}{8}$	3½ × 5½
4 × 8	$3\frac{9}{16} \times 7\frac{1}{2}$	3½ × 7¼
4 × 10	$3\frac{9}{16} \times 9\frac{1}{2}$	3½ × 9¼

The finish floor is a key element to any decor. The floor establishes the mood or impression you want observers to have of a room. Consider the finish floor early in the planning stage. There are a wide range of materials to select from. Carpet might be a good choice for your expanded living room. Or you might prefer a hardwood strip floor, as seen in FIG. 5-1.

Most basements have a concrete slab for a floor. The following are some of the flooring materials that can be installed directly on a dry basement floor:

- Asphalt
- Vinyl-asbestos
- Vinyl
- Sheet vinyl
- Terrazzo
- Ceramic

Foam rubber-backed carpeting can be laid directly on below-grade concrete floors. It is more or less mildew proof and unaffected by a little water. The backing is non-skid, and since it is a heavy material, tacks or adhesives are not necessary to hold the carpet in place.

Indoor/outdoor carpeting can be installed over concrete and old floor tile surfaces. The carpet backing is made of a closed-pore type of vinyl or latex foam that keeps out moisture. Vinyl and asbestos floor coverings accumulate moisture when covered with carpet, and thus produce a musty odor and cause mildew stains.

5-1 Hardwood flooring offers beauty and staying power.

REMOVING EXISTING FLOOR COVERING

If it is necessary to remove existing flooring before installing a new, educate yourself. Removing some old coverings can be hazardous to your health.

Vinyl Sheets Do not sand your old resilient flooring, backing or lining felt. These products may contain asbestos fibers and inhaling asbestos dust might cause asbestosis or other serious illness. To remove old sheet vinyl flooring, cut the wear layer into narrow strips. Peel up the strips from the backing by pulling or rolling around a core. After removing the wear layer, scrape off the remaining felt with a scraper. *Do not* sand.

Resilient Tile Use a hand scraper or long-handled scraper to remove old resilient floor tile. You can also use the dry ice method.

Place dry ice inside a 2-x-2 wooden frame that does not have a bottom or top. Place a piece of burlap, carpet or some other insulating material over the frame. (Several layers of newspapers will do if nothing else is available). This slows the evaporation process of the dry ice while directing the freezing action downward. Attach a rope to the frame to help move it over the floor.

Let the frame sit on an area of tile for five minutes or more. The tile will freeze and become brittle. Use a scraper or brick chisel to remove the tile. If the tile does not readily snap loose, freeze it some more. While you are removing frozen tile, freeze adjoining areas.

You can also remove some areas of tile with heat, using a blow torch or small propane gas torch. Have a water supply on hand when using heat: fires can be started by this method.

Do not use solvents for the removal of asphalt adhesive residue. The solvents will carry the residue deep into the pores of a wood subfloor or into a concrete slab, and the residue will rise or bleed to the surface to damage the new flooring just about the time you've finished paying for the project. Use a grinder, such as a concrete or terrazzo grinder, to remove asphalt adhesive residue. Use wet sand with the grinder for more efficiency and to prevent the residue from clogging the grinding stones.

Instead of removing the old resilient floor covering, consider installing a ¼-inch-thick 4-x-8 foot tempered hardboard underlayment on top of the old floor covering. It might prove easier and more economical, as well as not destroying your patience.

You can install most sheet vinyl directly over any type of structurally sound subfloor whether it is above, on, or below grade. Certain types of sheet vinyl can also be installed over almost any type of existing floors, including:

- Asphalt
- Vinyl-composition
- Rubber
- Vinyl
- Sheet vinyl
- Linoleum
- Clay
- Marble
- Ceramic (unglazed)

Before installing new sheet vinyl, roughen the borders on all non-porous surfaces. Also, before installing sheet flooring over a worn tile floor, remove old, damaged tiles with a putty knife or a scraper. Also remove the adhesive, and apply new adhesive and a new tile. It does not matter if the new tile matches the old tile, as long as it is the same size and thickness.

COVERING THE BASEMENT FLOOR

Basement floors catch spills of all sorts of things: motor oils, paints, wax, shoe polish. When you plan to convert your basement, plan on some floor preparation.

A dry, smooth, dense concrete floor makes a good surface for resilient floor covering as well as for carpeting. The slab should be free of cracks, expansion joints, depressions, scale, and foreign deposits of any kind. You will want to remove all oil, wax, varnish, paint, etc., from the surface before putting down the new covering.

Removing Paint and Grime Trisodium phosphate (TSP) in hot water is good wash for removing dirt and grime from walls and concrete floors. Use a strong detergent or solvent to remove grease and oil residue. Scrape or wire-brush peeling or scaling paint. For large areas remove the paint by grinding and sanding. Clean any expansion joints, cracks or score marks, and fill with a latex underlayment mastic.

Rough Concrete Floors Use a terrazzo grinder and clean white sand to smooth rough concrete floors. To prevent dust, keep the sand and concrete wet during sanding. Do not soak the floor: it must be thoroughly dry before you install the flooring.

Neutralizing Concrete Floors Alkali-treated concrete floors must be neutralized before you can install resilient flooring. Spread a mixture of one part muriatic acid and eight parts water over the floor. Leave it at least an hour. Rinse well with clear water. Let the floor dry thoroughly before installing covering.

INSTALLING SLEEPER JOISTS

Occasionally a basement floor is too dirty to clean or too rough to smooth. Or some condensation may form on the floor from time to time and you would feel better if you did not install the new floor covering directly on the concrete. The best alternative might be a sleeper joist system (FIG. 5-2).

Install a 6-mil polyethylene vapor barrier directly on top of the floor slab, overlapping the seams at least 6 inches. Seal the seams with a premium-quality acrylic latex caulking compound. Extend the vapor barrier up the walls a minimum of 3 inches. Lay the sleepers directly on the vapor barrier. Use pressure-treated 1 x 4s or 2 x 4s spaced 16 inches o.c. Anchor sleepers at each end with concrete nails.

Install the subfloor directly on the sleepers in the conventional manner, staggering panel end joints by at least one sleeper joist. Use ½-inch sheathing plywood or ⁷⁄₁₆-inch OSB panels.

Lay ⅝-inch-thick, 4-x-8 foot particle board panels on top of the subfloor panels so the edges and ends do not line up with the edges and ends of the subfloor panels. Space panels according to the manufacturer's recommendations.

You are now ready to install resilient floor covering or carpeting. For resilient flooring, use a grade of particle board floor underlayment manufactured for that purpose.

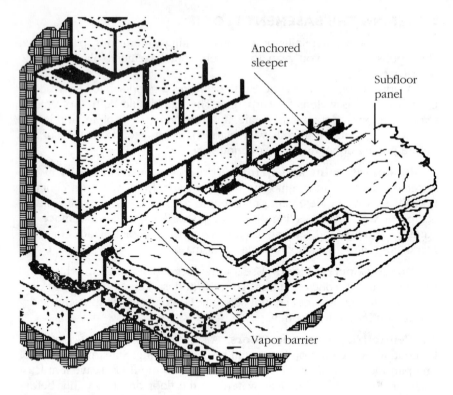

Anchored sleeper

Subfloor panel

Vapor barrier

5-2 Typical sleeper installation.

WOOD FLOORING

For permanence and attractiveness, wood flooring is hard to beat. Wood flooring is available in softwoods and hardwoods. Softwood flooring is made mostly from southern pine. Western hemlock, Douglas fir and larch are also used for softwood flooring. The flooring comes in various lengths and thicknesses, the most common size being 2¼ inches wide and ²⁵⁄₃₂ inch thick. Each board is tongued and grooved, and the underside is grooved to help reduce warping.

Oak and maple constitute most hardwood flooring. Other species used include beech, birch, hickory, and a few others. Hardwood flooring comes in ⅜, ½ and ²⁵⁄₃₂-inch thicknesses, in widths ranging from 1½ to 3¼ inches; the tongue and grooved 2¼-inch-wide strip is the most commonly used. Hardwood flooring is grooved on the back and the strips (boards) come in 2–16-foot lengths. Each board is end-matched (tongue and grooved).

Use a floor hammer when installing wood flooring. Flooring suppliers usually have hammers to rent. You can use a standard claw hammer to install the flooring, but a floor hammer makes the job easier.

Nail the strips down on underlayment or an existing floor. Install 15-pound felt over the underlayment before laying the floor. In new work, as

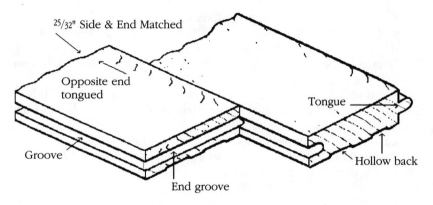

5-3 Fitting hardwood strip flooring.

in some attic conversions, apply the boards crosswise to the floor joists. If laying over an existing wood floor, install crosswise to old flooring. Figure 5-3 shows how to make the fit.

Wood flooring expands and contracts. When installing strip flooring, start the first strip at least ½ inch from the wall to allow for expansion, as shown in Fig. 5-4. Drive the face nail where the base or shoe mold will cover it. Then nail through the tongue, using cut flooring nails. (A floor hammer uses a special type nail).

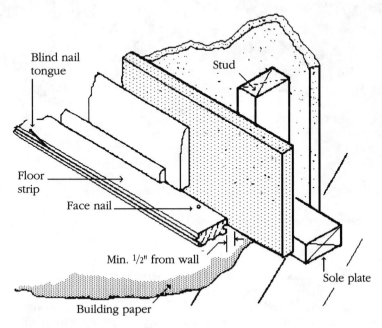

5-4 Nailing first floor board in place.

Nail remaining courses through tongues only until reaching the opposite wall where, it will be necessary to face-nail the last courses because you won't have room for hammer swing. Slant tongue nails at about a 45-degree angle when using a standard hammer (a floor hammer automatically sets the angle).

You do not want board ends to fall on a line: stagger the board butts. Crooked or warped boards are troublemakers—discard them. Leave a half-inch expansion space between the last course and the wall. Any increase in the moisture content of the floor will cause it to expand.

Hardwood blocks, such as parquet and laminated, are available in various sizes and thicknesses and can be some of the most expensive flooring.

SHEET VINYL FLOORING

Vinyl flooring is a good choice for bathrooms, kitchens, and playrooms, as well as for most other rooms. Figure 5-5 shows a pattern of sheet vinyl that works well for this redesigned bathroom.

Kemper Div. WCI, Inc.

5-5 Sheet vinyl makes an easy-to-maintain bathroom flooring.

Polyvinyl chloride (PVC) is the main ingredient of vinyl flooring. Resin binders with mineral fillers, plasticizers, stabilizers, and pigments are the other ingredients. Vinyl can be clear or filled. Clear vinyl consists of a layer of opaque particles or pigments covered with a wearing surface of clear vinyl bonded to vinyl or polymer-impregnated asbestos fibers or resin-saturated felt. Filled vinyl is made of chips of vinyl of different shapes and colors immersed in a clear vinyl base. All these ingredients are bonded by heat and pressure. As many homeowners can verify, the flooring has a high resistance to wear.

Whether you are installing sheet vinyl in the basement, attic, or in a room on the main floor, you want the best possible job you can get. The first step is to remove everything from the room that can be removed. Next, sweep and vacuum the area and drive in any protruding nail heads.

Look at FIG. 5-6. You want the flooring to slip easily under the doorway moldings; hold a handsaw flat on a piece of cardboard the same

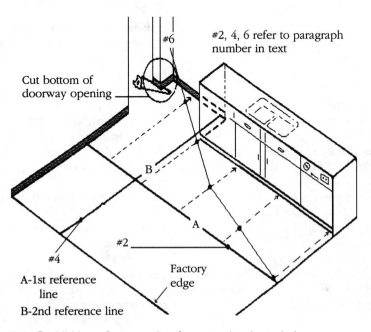

5-6 Establishing reference points for measuring sheet vinyl.

thickness as the flooring, and cut off the bottom of the moldings. To avoid errors cutting the flooring:

1. Select the wall against which you'll put one of the factory edges of the flooring. (The factory edges run the length of the flooring). You will want to place the factory edge along the longest straight wall.

2. Measure out from the selected wall to about the center of the room, at each end of the room (#2, FIG. 5-6).

3. Snap a chalk line through these two points. This is the first reference line.

4. Now mark a second line at a 90-degree angle to the first line at a point where the second line can run the entire width of the room. Be sure the line is exactly perpendicular to the first line. This is the

second reference line. The first and second reference lines now become the reference points from which to determine how to mark and cut the flooring (#4, FIG. 5-6).

5. Transfer the two reference lines to graph paper. Sketch the room around the intersection of the two lines. Include all offsets, such as cabinets and closets.

6. Carefully measure from the reference lines on the floor out to the walls or cabinet every two feet around the room. Do at least two measurements for every offset. Few walls are exactly straight, so measure every two feet (refer to #6, FIG. 5-6).

We want to position your floor plan sketch on the sheet vinyl so the first reference line is parallel to a factory edge of the flooring. Unroll the sheet vinyl face up, preferably in another room. Using the measurement written on your floor plan, measure in from the first reference line to the wall. Mark this distance at both ends of the sheet vinyl, and snap a chalk line through the points.

To establish the second reference line on the vinyl, measure along the first reference line from the edges to where the floor plan indicates the reference lines intersect. Snap a chalk line through the points at an exact 90-degree angle to the first line. This second line should run the entire width of the floor.

The vinyl is now marked with reference lines that match those in the room. Measure out from these lines to all walls and cabinets at the same intervals as shown on the floor plan you sketched on the graph paper. Connect these marks with a chalk line. These outside lines become your cut lines (FIG. 5-6).

Now go back and recheck all your measurements. If no mistakes were made, it is time to cut the flooring. Using a sharp utility knife and a straight-edge, cut along all outside cut lines. (Place plywood or cardboard beneath the cutting lines to avoid striking the floor underneath with the knife.)

Installation method for one-piece flooring

Before carrying the flooring into the room where it is to be installed, roll the vinyl face in, so it will roll out into the room along the longest straight wall.

Do not force the flooring under offsets or cabinets, but unroll enough to know that it is in the correct position. Fold half of the flooring back onto itself, being careful not to crimp the fold or to move the other half out of position. Spread the adhesive, following the manufacturer's instructions on the container. Spread the adhesive evenly, using a trowel with notches 1/16-inch wide, 1/16-inch deep and 3/32-inch apart. When the drying time specified by the adhesive's instructions has elapsed, place the flooring onto it.

Fold back the other half of the sheet vinyl and repeat the process. Use a heavy roller to ensure a good bond and remove air pockets. Roll from the center toward the edges.

Cap doorways and openings with a metal threshold strip. It is a common practice to carry the finish flooring material to the center of doorways and openings when different materials or patterns are used in the adjoining rooms. To do this, allow for half the width of the opening, and mark and cut the flooring accordingly.

Installation methods for two-piece flooring

A two-piece installation is necessary when the room has a side larger than 12 feet. Follow the procedures used for one-piece installation, with the following exceptions.

1. Overlap the two pieces at the seam area before transferring measurements onto the sheet vinyl. Be sure to match the pattern at the overlap.
2. Stick strips of masking tape across the overlap to hold the pieces together.
3. Transfer measurements onto the flooring and cut the vinyl to size and shape of the room. (Do not cut overlap seams.)
4. Remove tape from the seam and move the flooring to the room where it is to be installed.
5. Put both pieces in place—do one piece at a time.
6. Fold back the top piece halfway, and draw a pencil line on the subfloor along the edge of the bottom piece at seam area (FIG. 5-7).
7. Fold back the bottom piece and spread adhesives and spread adhesive to within 12 inches of either side of the line, as shown in FIG. 5-7.
8. Place the flooring in the adhesive and repeat steps 6 and 7 for the other half of the room.

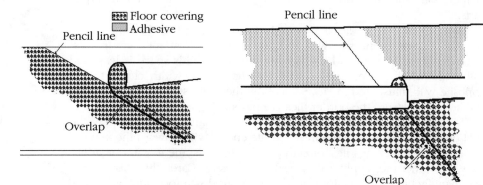

5-7 Overlap for two-piece installation.

9. Cut through both pieces at the overlap. Use a straight-blade utility knife and a metal straight-edge as a guide. You want a clean, straight cut.

10. Fold back both seams, spread adhesive, and place the vinyl into position.

Seam sealing is the last step when installing most vinyl sheet flooring. There are some floor coverings, however, in which seam sealing is one of the first steps. Determine this from your supplier and follow manufacturer's instructions.

Another way to install sheet vinyl flooring is to unroll the flooring in the room, extend the surplus up the walls, and trim in place.

VINYL TILE FLOORING

Vinyl tile makes an attractive and durable floor covering. Vinyl tile is made from polyvinyl chloride resins, pigment, and clay-based inert fillers. Sizes are 9 × 9 inch and 12 × 12 inch with thickness of $\frac{1}{16}$, $\frac{3}{32}$, or $\frac{1}{8}$ inch. Vinyl tile, like sheet vinyl, is in the resilient flooring category. Resilient flooring is nonrigid. Ceramic tile, terrazzo, stone, etc., are rigid.

Vinyl tile is available in various patterns and textures. It is semiflexible, and offers good resistance to oils, grease, alkaline substances and some acids. For best results, install the tile on a clean, smooth, rigid subfloor. The tile works well on below-grade slabs. Tile with peel-and-stick backing is available.

Border tiles on opposite sides of the room should be the same width. If the border tile on one side of the room is 7 inches, the border tile on the opposite side of the room should be 7 inches. Also, the border tiles at both ends of the room should be the same size.

Start to lay out tile by locating the center of the room. You do this by measuring each wall at the floor line and establishing the midpoint. Snap a chalk line on the subfloor (or existing floor covering) across the center of the room and then down the center of the room to get four equal parts.

As seen in FIG. 5-8, lay a row of loose tile along the chalk line from the center point to one side wall and one end wall. Now measure the distance between the wall and the last full tile at B. If this space is less than half a tile width, snap a new chalk line half a tile width closer to the opposite wall, illustrated in FIG. 5-9. Follow the same steps for row A. This will help you ensure the border tiles are not small pieces.

Lay the A-B rows first, then the rest of the quarter section. To lay the next quarter, begin where the installed tile ends, laying toward the walls.

Apply self-sticking tiles directly to the underlayment without adhesives. For other tile, apply a thin coat of adhesive. Carefully follow adhesive manufacturer's instructions: it is easy to put down too much adhesive, which can create a problem by continually seeping up through the tile. Do not slide the tile into place—this causes the adhesive to pile up at the joint. Lay the tile down flat and firmly.

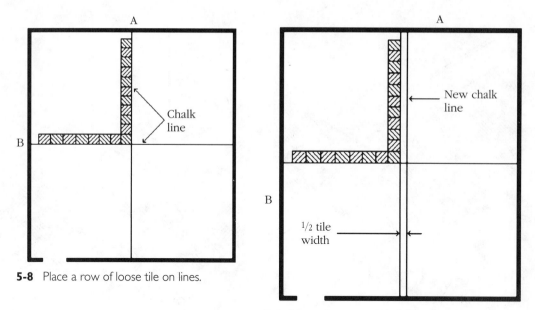

5-8 Place a row of loose tile on lines.

5-9 Move tiles to new chalk line.

To cut and fit the tile next to the wall, place a loose tile (A, in FIG. 5-10) squarely on top of the last full tile closest to the wall. Using the edge of the top tile as a guide, mark the tile under it, A, with a pencil. Cut tile A at the pencil line. Follow the same procedure for marking and cutting tile for corners and irregular shapes, as in FIG. 5-11.

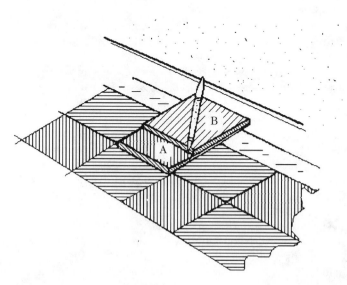

5-10 Measuring wall border tile.

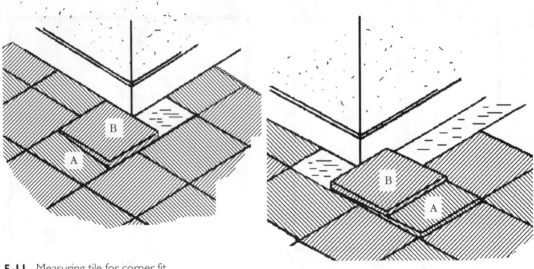

5-11 | Measuring tile for corner fit.

CERAMIC TILE

Not many do-it-yourselfers will want to tackle ceramic tile installation. Special tools are required and it is not something one learns to do on a weekend.

Ceramic tile has been around for centuries. It is made from natural clays and finely ground ceramic materials such as quartz, marble, silica, feldspar, fluxes, cements, pigments or acetylene black. The powders are either pressed to the desired shape or mixed with water and formed. Heat fuses the particles into a hard, solid mass.

Ceramic tile comes in glazed and unglazed surfaces. A glazed tile surface is made with a glass-like substance fused to the body of the tile when it's fired. Glazed tile is available in impervious porcelain, vitrified natural clay, quarry tile, nonvitreous white bodies; and comes in many sizes. Ordinary glazed wall tile has an impervious glaze over a white nonvitreous body.

Unglazed ceramic tile mosaics are manufactured in small 1×1 inch and 2-x-2 inch squares, 2-x-1 inch rectangles, 2-inch hexagonal shapes, and so on. They're used for floors, walls, countertops, fireplaces, decor, etc.

Unglazed quarry tile is made by the extrusion process from selected natural clays or shale. It is dense, coarse grained, and available in several solid colors. Quarry tile is generally 6 square inches or more. It is available in from ½–¾-inch-thick tiles.

Ceramic tile makes an ideal kitchen and bathroom floor. It is attractive and durable. If your project is redesigning your kitchen, think of matching ceramic tile countertops and backsplash with ceramic tile floor (FIG. 5-12). Colored tiles may be used to coordinate counter and floor colors (FIGS. 5-13 and 5-14).

American Olean Tile Co.

5-12 Ceramic tile can be a useful material when redesigning kitchens.

CARPETING

Wall-to-wall carpeting may be the ticket that puts your conversion or redesign project into a class all its own. Wall-to-wall carpeting provides some insulation and sound reduction. Carpet is available in outdoor, indoor, indoor/outdoor and artificial grass varieties. All carpets consist of a surface pile and a backing material. The surface pile may be wool, cotton, acrylic, polyester, or polypropylene. Most carpets come in 12-foot widths and are available in almost any lengths.

American Olean Tile Co.

American Olean Tile Co.

5-13 and 5-14 Coordinate ceramic tile colors for counter tops and floor.

Leave wall-to-wall carpet installation to the professionals. Installation charges are reasonable and you don't run the risk of angering your spouse because of a wrong cut or fit.

Wall-to-wall carpeting is commonly sold by the square yard. To find the square yards needed, multiply the length in feet by the width in feet and divide by 9. If your attic conversion is 12×18, the computation is:

$$12 \times 18 = 216 \div 9 = 24 \text{ square yards}$$

Padding or underlay extends carpet life, increases sound reduction and, of course, is more comfortable underfoot. One-piece and cushion-backed carpeting requires no additional padding or underlay. Vinyl foam, sponge-rubber foam, latex (rubber), and felted cushions made of animal hair or a combination of hair and jute are common types of padding. Latex and vinyl foams are considered the most practical. Their waffled surface helps to grip the carpet in place. Standard padding is 54 inches wide.

Cushion-backed and one-piece carpeting needs no extra padding or underlay. Foam rubber-backed carpeting is more or less mildew proof and is unaffected by water. It works well in basements and below grade on concrete floors. It is a heavy material and therefore stays in place without being glued or tacked. The backing is non-skid.

Indoor/outdoor carpeting works well over concrete and tile floors. The carpet's backing is made of a closed-pore vinyl or latex foam that helps to keep out moisture.

Do not install carpeting over vinyl or asbestos floor covering—these floorings will accumulate moisture when covered with carpet. The moisture soaks through into the carpet and eventually causes a musty odor and mildew stains.

MATERIALS AND LABOR HOURS

For your wood floor project, estimate materials and labor as follows:

Floor Boards (size)	Coverage (per 1000 B.F.)	Nails (pounds per 100 S.F.)
$^{25}/_{32}$" × 2"	702	3
$^{25}/_{32}$" × 2¼"	723	3
$^{25}/_{32}$" × 3¼"	775	2.3

A professional can lay about 1000 board feet (B.F.) of $^{25}/_{32}$ × 2¼-inch boards in 12 hours. A typical do-it-yourselfer might do the job in 36 hours.

As shown in the above chart, 1000 B.F. will cover 723 square feet. A 12 × 12 foot room is 144 square feet and will require 198 B.F. of 2¼-inch strips. You should lay the floor in about 7 hours. Sanding and finishing will take additional hours. Sanding will take from 2 to 3 hours per 100 square feet, depending upon your ability to handle a floor sander. Figure filling holes and two coats of lacquer at 3 hours per 100 square feet.

Your resilient tile needs are found by dividing the square inches of the room by tile square inches. This gives the number of tiles needed. Add 10 percent for cutting and waste. Let's do an example using a 12 × 16 room, which is 192 square feet. To find the square inches in 192 square feet, multiply 192 by 144 (the square inches in a square foot).

$$192 \times 144 = 27648 \text{ square inches} \div 81$$
$$(9 \times 9 \text{ inch tile size}) = 341.3 \text{ pieces.}$$

Add 10 percent for cutting and waste for a total of 375 tile.

A professional can lay 9 × 9 inch vinyl tile at 1.5 hours per 100 square feet. Allow yourself 3 to 4 hours for 100 square feet if it is your first time installing tile.

Sheet vinyl is available in 6-foot and 12-foot widths. Determine flooring requirements on the basis of the room size and cut-outs for obstructions such as cabinets. A 16 × 18 foot room without obstructions will require 288 square feet of sheet flooring, plus about 2 inches at each wall to allow for any adjustments due to off-square walls.

An experienced installer can put down 100 square feet of .070-inch-thick sheet vinyl in about 1.8 hours; two hours per 100 square feet for .090-inch-thick vinyl. The do-it-yourselfer will take twice as long to do the same job.

Chapter **6**

Dormers

A dormer can turn an otherwise unconvertible attic into additional living space. A dormer can add headroom, square footage, ventilation and natural light. Building a dormer is a major task—an undertaking only the more experienced do-it-yourselfer should contemplate.

Basically, there are two types of dormers—shed and gable (see FIG. 6-1). The shed dormer is commonly a back-of-the-house job, while the gable dormer fits nicely on the front of the house. This is not a law, and a shed dormer can be (and often is) built on the front part of the roof.

The house in FIG. 6-1 is essentially a one-story house because most of the rafters rest on the first-floor top plate. Space, light and ventilation are provided by the shed and gable dormers. Additional light and ventilation is gained at the gable end windows. Roof slopes for this style house (Cape Cod) can vary from 9 in 12 to 12 in 12, to provide the needed headroom.

DESIGNING THE CORRECT DORMER

For our purpose, a dormer is a framed structure projecting from a roof surface, as shown in FIGS. 6-2 and 6-5. It may be built up from the level of the house's top plate, or at a point beyond the top plate within the rafter span.

The dormer does not have to carry out the main roof line but usually does, because most dormers are built for appearances only. In the case of attic conversions, the dormer is constructed to provide natural light, ventilation, space and headroom, and as a possible point of exit in case of an emergency. A dormer is, comparatively, a low-cost way to gain valuable space in a critical area. In many cases, the dormer makes it possible to convert an attic.

To maintain the proper balance, at least two dormers placed an equal distance from the ends of the house are recommended. On long houses three dormers may be required from an aesthetic point of view. The center dormer should be located exactly in the center of the house for balance. We all have seen houses where the center dormer was off-center; as

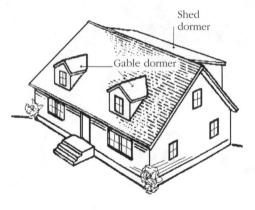

6-1 Types of dormers.

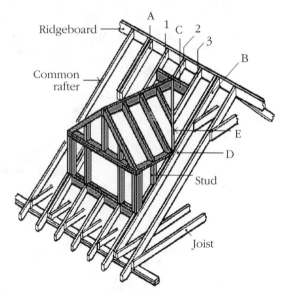

6-2 Dormer framing.

in most rules of design, there are always exceptions due to roof layout and house design—as well as individual preferences. In some cases, one large gable dormer might be preferred to two smaller ones.

Determine the exact location of the dormer and ceiling height. The ceiling may be the same height as or lower than the main attic ceiling. A dormer ceiling may be vaulted, or conventional with ceiling joists. (More about attic ceilings in Chapter 10.)

Look at FIG. 6-2—it shows the framing. (The roofing and roof sheathing of the main roof are not shown.) The roofing and sheathing of the main roof must first be removed in the area where the dormer will be built.

Cut rafters #1, #2, and #3. Rafter #2 may be cut at the point even with your conversion's vaulted ceiling height, which we will assume is 8 feet. Allow an additional 1½ inches for the thickness of the header, C. Cut rafter #2. This is a plumb cut you can ascertain with a level.

To determine where to cut the lower end of rafters #1, #2, and #3, mark the interior face of the dormer's front wall as shown in FIG. 6-3. Using a level, mark a plumb line on rafter #2. Add 3½ inches for the thickness of the window sill frame and mark the plumb cut. Cut rafters #1 and #3 at the same point.

Figures 6-2 and 6-4 show the dormer wall height (from floor to top of dormer top plate). Snap a chalk line on top of rafters from D plumb to the juncture at header C and the dormer ridge board position, shown in FIG. 6-4. This gives the miter cut for rafter #3 (and any additional rafters between D and C.) Use a level to mark plumb cut at miter line. Repeat the

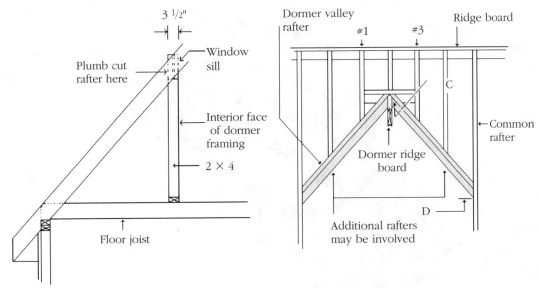

6-3 Cutting lower end of rafters.

6-4 Making plumb and miter cuts for dormer.

above steps to find the miter and plumb cuts for rafter #1 and others. The dormer valley rafters will fit flush against the cut rafters.

You will note in FIG. 6-2 that the dormer is constructed between main roof rafters A and B, a distance of 4 rafters spaced 16 inches o.c. The dormer width is 62½ inches. If you allow 6 inches for wall space on each side of the window (which gives the window a nice border appearance on the outside and adequate space inside for hanging drapes) you'll have a 50½-inch window space.

If possible, plan your dormer width to fit between existing common rafters. Reinforce the roof by doubling the rafter at each side wall (A and B), as pictured in FIG. 6-2. You can rest the dormer side wall studs and the short valley rafter on the double rafter. Or, you can carry the dormer side wall studs past the double rafter to rest on a sole plate nailed to the dormer subfloor.

The shed dormer commonly appears at the rear of the house. It is almost always centered, again, there are exceptions. The shed dormer is less complicated to build than the gable dormer. Figure 6-5 shows a typical framing method for a shed dormer. When using wood shingles on shed dormers, give the rafters a 6-inch rise to the foot so they will properly shed rain and snow.

Determine the dormer ceiling height for shed dormers as for gable dormers. Mark the existing house rafters at the dormer header position for a vertical (plumb) cut. Before cutting rafters for a dormer opening, install temporary braces to support the roof. Cut rafters at header position. Measure and cut the lower rafter end (at front dormer wall) the same as for gable dormers, as explained above.

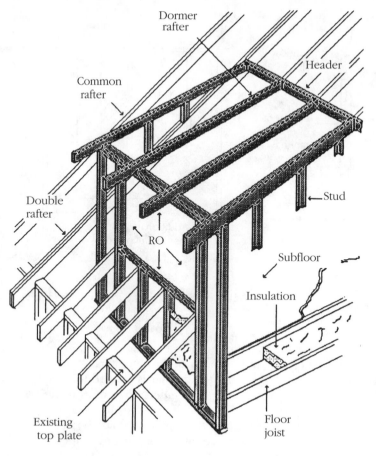

6-5 Shed dormer components.

Install a header as shown in FIG. 6-5. Use a double header on spans greater than 4 feet (FIG. 6-6). Face-nail the header to the cut rafters with three 16d nails at each rafter.

You are now ready to proceed: Build the front wall section of the dormer. The studs, plates, and window openings are framed and erected as an outside wall. If the attic is floored, put the wall together on the floor. Space the studs so the lower rafter ends will fit against the studs, as shown in FIG. 6-5. When the wall is raised and plumbed into place, nail the sole plate to the floor joists through the subfloor with 16d nails. Face-nail the lower rafter ends to the studs with three 12d nails to each rafter.

Lay out and cut the required number of dormer rafters. Install the rafters. Toenail the rafters to the dormer top plate (front wall) with two 10d nails or secure with metal rafter ties. Secure the dormer rafters to the header you installed on the main rafters. Double the main common rafters on each side of the dormer with same-size stock.

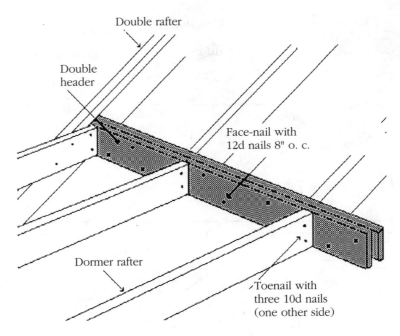

Double rafter

Double header

Face-nail with
12d nails 8" o. c.

Dormer rafter

Toenail with
three 10d nails
(one other side)

6-6 Use double header for spans over 4 feet.

Angle cut the dormer sidewall studs to fit on top of the double rafter and under the dormer end rafter as shown in FIG. 6-5. The alternative method is to extend the stud from the sole plate to the dormer rafter, nailing the stud to the house rafter at the point of contact. Space sidewall dormer studs 16 inches or 24 inches o.c. Nail on the roof and wall sheathing and apply roof covering. Complete dry-in by installing window.

HOW TO MEASURE AND CUT RAFTERS

Now we are going to get a little complicated—perhaps not for you, but for me. Measuring and cutting rafters is an exact science and when it is done right, everything fits exactly as it should. The first requirement is that the building or dormer be square.

Rafters make up the main body of the frame in all pitched roofs. There are several kinds of rafters—common, hip, valley, jacks, etc. Figure 6-7 illustrates various roof components and terminology. The run of a rafter is the level, or horizontal, distance from the outside of the wall plate to the point straight under the ridge. The run of the rafter is one-half the span of the roof.

The rise of a rafter is the vertical distance from the top of the wall plate to the measuring line on the ridge. To figure the rise, calculate the distance from the top of the plate line to the point where the measuring line meets the ridge board. We usually include the overhang in the overall length of the rafter (see FIG. 6-8).

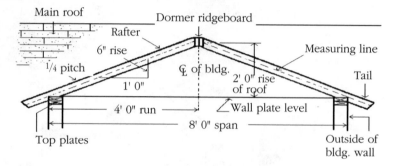

6-7 Definition of roof and rafter terms.

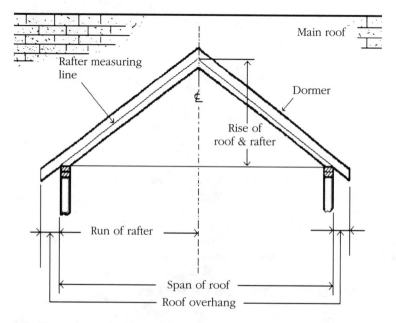

6-8 Rise and run of rafter—gable roof.

The roof span is the distance between the outside edge of the wall plates that support the rafters. In a gable roof with a centered ridge, the roof span is twice the run of a rafter. Figure 6-9 shows the run, rise, and span for a shed room.

The pitch of a roof is the slope or angle from ridge to plate. Because this slope changes if the rise (height of ridge) or span changes, it is expressed as *a ratio of the rise to the span.* For example, a ⅓ pitch roof means the rise is ⅓ of the span, and ¼ pitch means that the rise is ¼ of the span (see FIGS. 6-10 and 6-11).

You can determine the pitch this way: in FIG. 6-7 the rise is 2 feet and the span 8 feet, so the ratio is 2 to 8. Reduce this to a smaller fraction by dividing both numbers by the common denominator 2, which gives us ¼. Thus, we have a ¼ pitch.

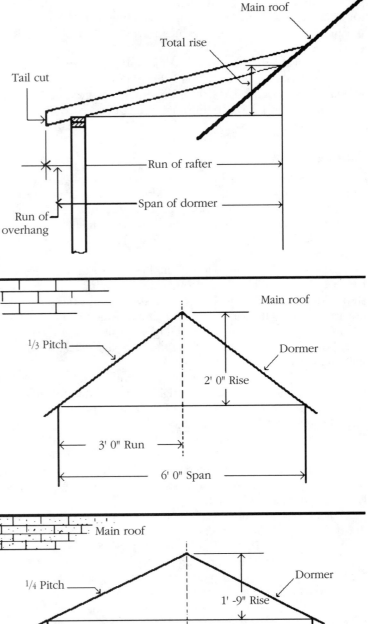

6-9 Shed roof details—rise and run of rafter.

Main roof

Total rise

Tail cut

Run of rafter

Span of dormer

Run of overhang

6-10 One-third pitch.

Main roof

¹/₃ Pitch

Dormer

2' 0" Rise

3' 0" Run

6' 0" Span

6-11 One-quarter pitch.

Main roof

¹/₄ Pitch

Dormer

1' -9" Rise

3' -6" Run

7' 0" Span

The pitch of a roof may also be described as the increase in the rise for each foot of run. For example, a slope may be 6 inches per foot, meaning that a rafter rises 6 inches for every foot of run—the horizontal distance covered.

The roof overhang, also called the *eave* or *rafter* tail, is the lower end of the rafter that extends beyond the building line. This length must be added to the calculated length of the rafter. If rafter ends will be enclosed by a cornice, you'll have to finish cut the tail end accordingly.

Cutting rafters

There are several ways to find the length and cuts of roof rafters. The same rules apply whether the rafters are long house rafters or short dormer rafters. The basic principle of all methods is geometric construction (trigonometry). Each of the three common methods—the graphic, the rafter table (printed on most steel framing squares), and the step-off—works well.

Carpenters find the step-off method or the rafter table convienent because the procedure is laid out with a framing square. If you use the step-off method you can check your results against the rafter table.

Lay out all rafters in the same relative position in order to avoid confusion. Crown each board by sighting along it to find the bow, if there is one. You want the bow on the top side of the rafter, so place the board with the crowned edge (top) toward you.

Hold the tongue (short leg) of the framing square in your left hand and the body (long leg) in your right hand. In this mannner, the tongue will form the vertical, or top, cut of the rafter and the body will form the level, or seat cut (shown in FIG. 6-12).

Use your square to find the approximate length of a common rafter. The rise of the rafter (in feet) is represented on the tongue of the square. The run (in feet) is represented on the body. Measure the length of the diagonal between these two points. The measurement, expressed in feet, is the rough length of the rafter.

For example, assume that the total rise of your dormer is 4 feet and the run is 3 feet. Find 4 and 3 on the square (FIG. 6-13) and measure the diagonal distance. This will be 5 feet. If there is a cornice overhang, add the overhang length. In our example above, the rafter length is 5 feet. If the overhang is 12 inches, you'll need 6-foot stock. (A 12-foot board will provide two rafters).

You should make the first pattern rafter out of straight stock of the correct rough length. Lay the board flat across two sawhorses and place the square near the right-hand end (see FIG. 6-14).

The 12-inch mark on the outside edge of the body (representing the run of the roof), and the inch mark on the outside edge of the tongue that represents the rise of the roof, should both come at the edge of the rafter. This is the top edge (see points A and F in FIG. 6-14). Draw the line AB on the board to mark the top of the wall plate. Then measure 3⅝" along this line, from B to C, to find the outside top corner of the plate. This must be

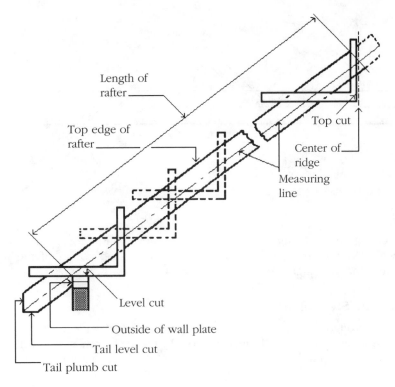

6-12 Common rafter layout—step-off method.

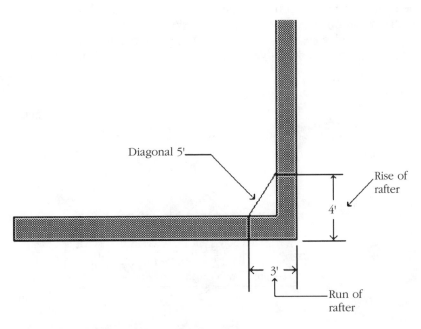

6-13 Finding the rough length of a rafter.

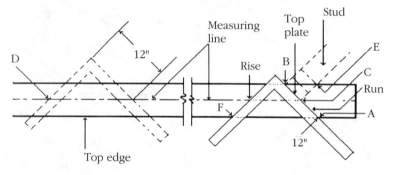

6-14 Locating rafter measuring line.

far enough from the right-hand end of the rafter to allow for the tail (overhang). The measuring line runs from the outside top corner of the wall plate along the rafter, parallel to the edge, CD.

Lay Out: Step-off method

To go through this process, we'll use a dormer 6 feet wide with the pitch of the rafter being ⅔, or 16-inch rise on 12 inches of run which will give the dormer roof a total rise of 4 feet. To find the exact length of the rafter, do this:

Lay the square on the board so the 12-inch mark on the outside of the body is at point C (FIG. 6-15). Put the 16-inch mark on the outside edge of the tongue on the measuring line at E. Be sure these two marks are exactly on the measuring line. Mark along the outside edges of the square's tongue and body. Find point E on the measuring line. Slide the square to the left until the 12-inch mark is over E (position 2 in FIG. 6-15) and again mark

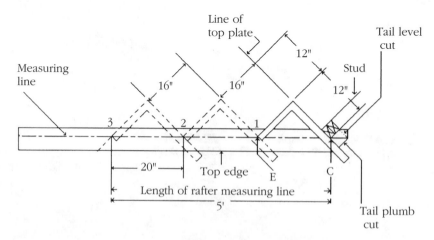

6-15 Laying out the dormer common rafter with step-off method.

along the tongue and body. Do this as many times as there are feet run of the rafter (three in this case). Upon reaching the last position, draw a line along the tongue across the rafter to mark the centerline of the ridge board.

Lay Out: For an odd span

Assume your dormer is 7 feet wide, an odd number. The pitch of the rafter is ⅔, or 16-inch rise on a 12-inch run. The run of the rafter will be half the width of the dormer, or 3 feet 6 inches.

Lay out this rafter the same as the one just described, except at the end you'll take an extra half step for the added 6 inches of rafter. After the third step is marked, put the square on the top edge of the rafter, shown in FIG. 6-16. Now move the square until the 6 on the outside of the body is right over line A from the third step. Draw a line along the outside edge of the tongue. This is the centerline of the ridge board.

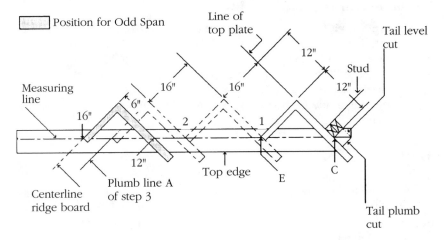

6-16 Laying out an additional half-step.

Allow for the ridge board

The last line marked on the rafter shows where you would cut the rafter if all rafters were to be butted against each other instead of the ridge board. Since most stick-built roofs have a ridge board, the rafter we just laid out will be a bit too long. The solution is to cut a piece off the end of the rafter. This piece will be equal to half the thickness of the ridge board, as shown in FIG. 6-17.

To lay out this cutting line, measure half the thickness of the ridge board at a right angle to the last line (position 3 in FIG. 6-15). Now slide the square back for this distance. Mark the plumb cut along the outside edge of the tongue. This line should be inside of, and parallel to, the original line marking the rafter's end.

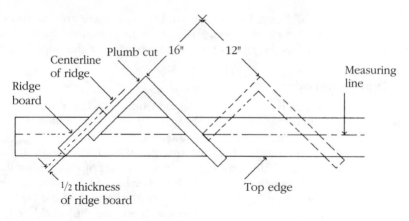

6-17 Making allowance for ridgeboard.

The bottom or seat cut

Almost every do-it-yourselfer has heard the term *birdsmouth* pertaining to rafters. This is the bottom or seat cut of the rafter and is a combination of the level (—) and plumb (|) cuts. The level cut (BC, FIG. 6-14) rests on the top face of the side wall top plate. The plumb cut (CE, FIG. 6-14) fits against the outside edge of the side wall top plate. You lay out the plumb cut by squaring a line from line AB (FIG. 6-14) through point C. This is CE, and represents the plumb cut.

The tail

If your dormer's rafter tail is the kind shown in FIG. 6-15, make the cut along the measuring line as shown. Find the level cut at the end of the tail by sliding the square toward the tail. Mark the rafter where the body of the square crosses both the plumb and measuring line.

If the dormer will have a box cornice as seen in FIG. 6-18 lay out the level and plumb cuts as before, making allowance for the thickness of the wall sheathing because it extends into the rafter notch up to the top of the top plate. To do this, lay out line AB parallel to line CD. Make it the thickness of the sheathing away from CD. Then extend the line of the level cut at D to meet AB. The rafter will now fit over the plate and sheathing.

If a 12-inch piece will be used at E, continue the line of the level cut through B to F on the top edge of the rafter. Lay the body of the square along this line. Put the 12-inch mark on the outside edge directly over point B. Mark a line GH along the outer edge of the tongue across the rafter. The tip of the rafter is at the point where this line meets the measuring line at H. Square the line HJ across the rafter from line GH to locate J.

Jack rafters

Your dormer has two jack rafters. It also has two valley rafters, which you added after cutting existing house common rafters. Jack rafters lie in the

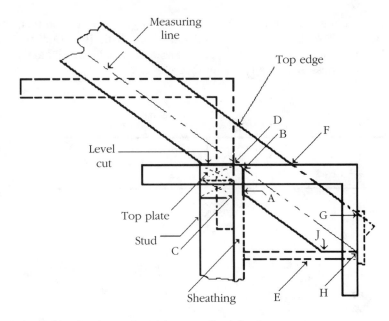

6-18 Use framing square to lay out rafter tail cut.

same plane with common rafters, and are spaced the same, and have the same pitch. They also have the same length per foot run as common rafters.

In reality, the dormer jack rafters are no more than discontinued common rafters cut off by the intersection of the valley rafter. Jack rafters are spaced the same as common rafters, 16 or 24 inches o.c. and as the jack rests against the valley rafter equally spaced, the second jack (when there is more than one) must be twice as long as the first jack rafter. If there is a third jack, it will be three times longer than the first and so on.

To find the length of jack rafters, go to your framing square. The lengths of jacks are given in the third and fourth line of the rafter tables printed on the body and are indicated:

3rd line: "Difference in length of jacks—16 inches centers"
4th line: "Difference in lengths of jacks—2 feet centers"

The figures in the table indicate the length of the first or shortest jack, which is also the difference in lengths between the first and second, between second and third, between third and fourth, etc. Here's the rule:

"To find the length of a jack rafter, multiply the value given in the tables by the number indicating the position of the jack. From the obtained length subtract half the diagonal (45-degree) thickness of the valley rafter."

Let's do an example that finds the length of the first jack rafter. The dormer roof has a rise of 16 inches to one foot of run of common rafter; the spacing of jacks are 16 inches o.c. Pick up your square. On the outer edge of the body find figure 16, which corresponds to the rise of the roof.

On the third line under this figure find 26¹¹⁄₁₆. This means that the first jack rafter will be 26¹¹⁄₁₆ inches. The second jack rafter, if there is one, will be double this figure, or 53⅜ inches. Now we deduct half the diagonal (45 degrees) thickness of the valley rafter (see FIG. 6-19).

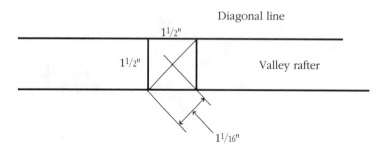

6-19 Half the 45-degree thickness of a 1½ inch thick board is equal to 1¹⁄₁₆ inch.

Jack rafters have the same rise per foot as common rafters, thus, the method of obtaining the top and bottom cuts is the same as for common rafters—take 12 inches on the body of the square and the rise per foot run on the tongue, which for our dormer would be 16 inches. The 12 inches on the body will give the seat cut, and the 16 inches on the tonue will give the plumb cut (see FIG. 6-15).

At the top end of the jack rafter we make a plumb cut to fit the ridge board. At the bottom end we make a side, or cheek, cut to fit to the valley rafter. The side cuts for jacks is found on the fifth line of the rafter table, printed on the framing square marked "Side cut of jacks—use." Here's the rule: To obtain the side cut for a jack rafter take the figure shown in the table on the body of the square and 12 inches on the tongue. Mark along the tongue for the side cut.

Let's do an example and find the side cut for the jack rafter in our dormer, which has a roof rise of 16 inches per foot run, which is a ⅔ pitch. Under the figure 16 in the fifth line of the table find 7³⁄₁₆. This figure, taken on the outside of the edge of the body and 12 inches on the tongue, will give the desired side cut (see FIG. 6-20).

INSTALLING ROOF SHEATHING

You'll want the roof sheathing to be thick enough to carry the roofing material and snow and ice loads between the supports. Plywood (½-inch thick) or OSB (⁷⁄₁₆-inch thick) panels installed on rafters spaced 16 or 24 inches o.c. will do the job in most areas.

Lay sheathing panels with the long dimension perpendicular to the rafters. Stagger the end joints. Nail with 8d box nails at each bearing, 6 inches apart along all edges and 12 inches apart along intermediate mem-

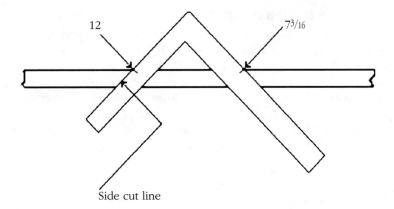

12   7³/₁₆

Side cut line

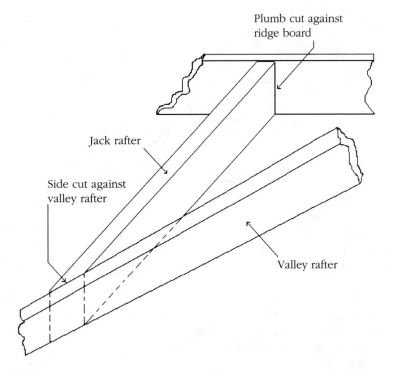

Plumb cut against
ridge board

Jack rafter

Side cut against
valley rafter

Valley rafter

6-20 Establishing the side cut of a jack rafter and fitting the jack rafter into position.

bers. Unless the panels have an exterior glue line, the bare edge should not be exposed to the weather at the gable (rake) or at the eaves. Use a metal drip cap at edges.

When installing sheathing panel leave a ⅛-inch edge spacing and ¹⁄₁₆-inch end spacing for expansion. Apply 15-pound felt (building paper) underlayment to dry-in the roof.

SHINGLING A DORMER ROOF

During dormer construction have on hand ample polyethylene with which to protect the attic from weather. For our dormer roof we are going to use what is called an open valley. While it is not necessary to re-roof the main house, it is necessary that the shingles joining the dormer be removed or loosened. Step flashing is recommended at dormer side walls (see FIG. 6-21). Valley flashing is recommended at thedormer valley. The step flashing and valley flashing must be free to slip under exisiting roofing.

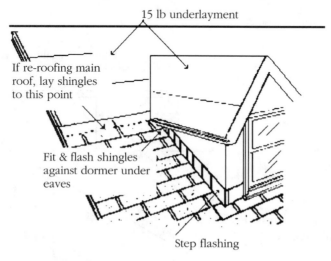

6-21 Before valley work can begin, main roof shingles must be laid, up to lower end of dormer valley.

Roof planes that butt against vertical walls are best protected by metal flashing shingles placed over the end of each shingle course. This is called step flashing. The metal flashing shingles are rectangular, 10 inches long and 7 inches wide, 2 inches wider than the exposed face of the roofing shingles. Here's how it works: when used with strip shingles with a 5-inch exposure, 5 inches extend over the roof deck and 5 inches extend up the wall. Each flashing unit is placed just up the roof from the exposed edge of the shingle that will overlap it so it will not be visible when the overlapping shingle is in place. Figure 6-22 shows application details.

The typical do-it-yourselfer is never surprised by the many details that can go into what might appear to be a simple project. Sometimes, the details are complex and extensive. Often it is necessary to go back over instructions several times before things begin to make any sense. No one should expect to understand rafter measuring and cutting on the first reading.

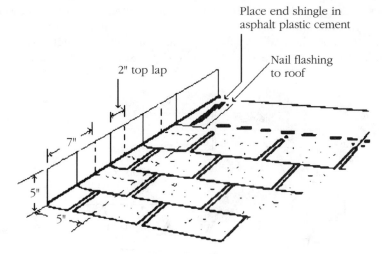

Place end shingle in asphalt plastic cement

Nail flashing to roof

2" top lap

7"

5"

5"

6-22 Installing metal step flashing.

When installing step flashing, it is essential to follow these steps to guard against leaks:

1. Place the flashing unit over the end of the first shingle at the dormer wall, and position it so the tab of the end shingle in the next course covers it completely.

2. Temporarily secure the horizontal arm (or tab) of the flashing unit to the roof by tacking it with a roofing nail. (The dormer front wall flashing will extend around the corner and fit under this step.) Do not nail the flashing to the dormer wall.

3. Position the second step flashing strip in the next shingle course and make sure the shingle completely covers it. You do not want any horizontal portion of the flashing to stick out from under the shingle. Fasten the horizontal arm to the roof. Continue in the same manner up the roof for the complete distance of the side wall. The metal flash strip is 7 inches wide and the roof shingles are laid with a 5-inch exposure. Each flashing course will overlap the course below by about 2 inches.

When the dormer front wall has been flashed you'll bring the dormer siding down over the vertical sections of the step flashing to serve as a cap flashing. Do not bring wood siding down against the roofing. Leave room to paint the siding.

At the point where the front dormer wall extends through the roof, trim a course of shingles to fit at the base of the vertical wall. Apply a continuous piece of metal flashing over the last course of shingles by embedding it in asphalt plastic cement and nailing it to the roof with roofing nails.

Use a 26-gauge metal flashing strip bent to extend at least 5 inches up the vertical wall and at least 4 inches onto the last shingle course. Do not nail the strip to the wall. Apply an additional row of shingles over the metal flashing strip, trimmed to the width of the strip (see FIG. 6-23).

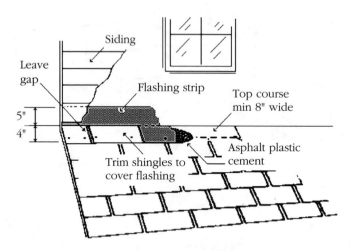

Siding

Leave gap

Flashing strip

Top course min 8" wide

5"
4"

Asphalt plastic cement

Trim shingles to cover flashing

6-23 Installing flashing against dormer front wall.

Cut the flashing so it extends at least 7 inches around the corner and under the wall step flashing. The front wall flashing may be installed before side wall step flashing. Bring the siding down over the vertical flashing to serve as cap flashing. Leave room between wood siding and shingles so you can paint. Do not nail siding into front or step flashing. This lets the flashing shift freely in the event the dormer or roof settles.

DORMER ROOF VALLEY FLASHING

Because there is a valley between a dormer and main roof, first things must be done first. If you're re-roofing, do not install valley flashing until the shingle application reaches a point just above the lower end of the valley, as shown in FIG. 6-21.

Begin by centering a 18-inch-wide strip of 15-pound felt in the valley. Use only enough roofing nails along the outer edges to hold it in place. Lay the first layer of valley flashing centerways of the valley. Use 18-inch-wide, 90-pound mineral-surfaced roll roofing. Install it with the mineral surface down by pressing it into the valley, and nailing it at the edge. Use only enough roofing nails to hold it in place.

Center a second strip, 36 inches wide, in the valley over the first strip, mineral surface facing up. Nail the strip in place in the same manner as the first strip. Extend the bottom of the valley strip to project at least 2 inches below the point where the two roofs meet. Extend the upper portion so the portion on the main roof extends 18 inches above the point where the dormer intersects the main roof. Trim the portion on the dormer at the ridge. Figure 6-24 shows the details.

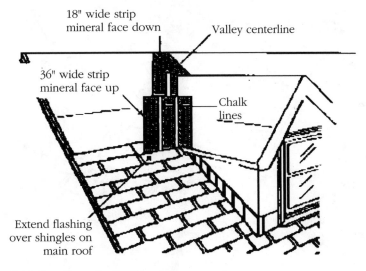

6-24 Installing valley flashing at dormer roof.

Now go to the valley on the other side and apply valley flashing the same way, extending the portion on the main roof up and over the portion from the first valley. Use a thin bead of asphalt plastic roofing cement to seal the seams and nail at the edges. Lap the valley flashing on the dormer side over the ridge, cement and nail.

You will have to trim the lower end of the top flashing piece on the dormer side to match the underlying 18-inch strip to extend ¼ inch over dormer eaves (FIG. 6-24). Trim the valley flashing that lies on the main roof to overlap the nearest course of shingles (FIG. 6-24). As you can see, this overlap is the same as the normal lap of one shingle over another. In our dormer we are using 12-inch-wide, three-tab strip shingles, so we extend the flashing to the top of the cutouts. Your next course of shingles will lay on top of the flashing and extend to the top of the same cutouts, covering the flashing. Trim the lower end of the flashing on a small radius arc that bridges slightly over the point of intersection between the dormer and main roof to allow for a smooth fit.

Snap chalk lines on the valley flashing 3 inches on each side of the valley centerline at the top and diverging ⅛ inch per foot to the bottom of the valley, thus making the valley wider at the bottom than at the top. Apply shingles, trimming the end shingle in each course to the chalk line. Clip the upper corner of the end shingle back about 1 inch and embed

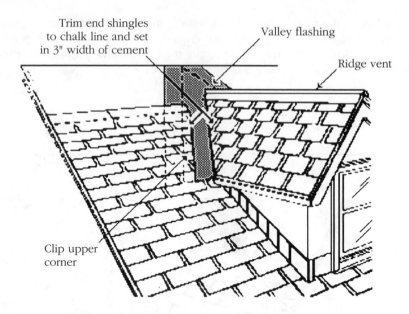

6-25 Completing shingle application.

the shingle in a 3-inch-wide strip of asphalt plastic cement to seal it to the flashing. (see FIG. 6-25).

Continue laying shingles on the dormer roof until the roof is covered. If you are not using a ridge vent, apply the dormer ridge shingles, starting at the front of the dormer and working toward the main roof. Apply the last ridge shingle so it extends at least 4 inches onto the main roof. Slit the center of the portion attached to the main roof and nail it in place. Apply the main roof course to cover the portion of the last ridge shingle on the main roof. Figure 6-26 shows how to cut a strip shingle to get pieces for the ridge. Figure 6-27 illustrates how ridge shingles are installed.

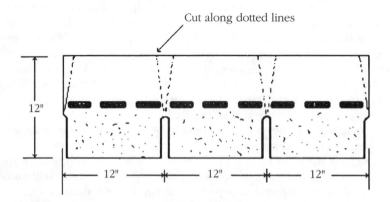

6-26 A three-tab strip shingle makes three ridge tabs.

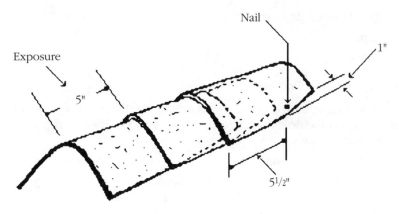

6-27 Installation of ridge shingle tabs.

General shingle application procedures for all strip shingles are about the same. There are differences, however, in applying the first course and in applying the first shingle in each course. Read the instructions supplied with each pack of shingles and begin your application accordingly.

ESTIMATING FRAMING MATERIALS AND LABOR HOURS

A dormer 6 feet wide with a 64-inch-long ridge, a ⅔ roof pitch, framed as shown in FIG. 6-2 will require:

Roof framing:
3 2 × 6 12 ft. (for 6 common rafters, 6 ft. long)
1 2 × 6   6 ft. (for 2 jack rafters, 26¹¹⁄₁₆ in. long)
1 2 × 6   6 ft. (for ridge board 64 in. long)
1 2 × 6   3 ft. (for header C)
2 2 × 6 10 ft. (for 2 valley rafters, 9.71 ft. long)
2 2 × 6 16 ft. (for double common rafters at A and B)
1 2 × 4 10 ft. (for gable end uprights)

Wall framing:
6 2 × 4 studs (for corner posts)
7 2 × 4 studs (for wall studs)
2 2 × 6   6 ft. (for window sill)
2 2 × 4 12 ft. (for top plates)

Roof materials
3 4' × 8'½-in. plywood (or ⁷⁄₁₆-in. OSB panels)
125 ft.² square feet 15-lb. felt
30 li. ft. 36-in.-wide 90-lb. roofing
3 gal. asphalt plastic cement
¾ square (75 ft.²) shingles for dormers plus house shingles
18 metal step flashing
8 ft. 9-in. metal flashing

20 li. ft. metal drip caps

Nails
2 lb. 10d
3 lb. 16d
2 lb. 1¼-in. roofing

Time estimates for dormer construction fall within a wide range, depending on the do-it-yourselfer's abilities and experience. A professional carpenter should complete the tasks in the following time:

Task	Hours
Dormer layout and roof opening dimensions	1
Removing shingles and cutting opening	4
Marking and cutting house rafters	2
Doubling two house rafters	1.5
Framing dormer front wall	4
Framing side walls to house rafters	1
Framing side walls to sole plate	2
Roof framing	3.5
Installing sheathing and felt	2.15
Valley preparation and roofing	3
Total	24.15

The typical do-it-yourselfer should do the job in approximately twice the time. Applying the siding, installing the window, cornice work, and trim will take another 24 hours.

Chapter 7

Closets

Regardless of how many closets there may be in the house, there never seems to be enough storage space. Most of us could benefit from a closet management course to help maintain closet discipline (FIG. 7-1). And let's not forget the kitchen, where cabinet clutter can become a major problem. Kitchen closets or cabinets can be designed to eliminate an assortment of storage problems and greatly increase one's efficiency in the kitchen (FIG. 7-2).

It wasn't too many years ago that few or no closets were built into houses except for the pantry. A chifforobe or wardrobe, pieces of furni-

7-1 Keeping closet order.

7-2 Ample storage space can increase efficiency.

ture, were used in lieu of closets. Today the size and placement of closets is covered by building codes. For example, each bedroom must have at least one closet with a depth of 2 feet, and at least 3 feet wide.

The first or lower shelf should not be more than 74 inches above the room floor. The closet must have at least one shelf and rod. An 8-inch clear space is required over the shelf. The floor of the closet should be finished and at least half the closet floor should be flat. Figures 7-3 and 7-4 illustrate these requirements.

A coat closet of the same minimum size and equipment as a bedroom closet is required. The coat closet should be near the living room and close to the front entrance.

You'll want to locate a linen closet near the bedrooms. Make the closet at least 14 inches deep, 18 inches wide, and space the shelves 1 foot apart. No shelf should be deeper than 24 inches nor higher than 74 inches. Plan for 9 square feet of shelf space for a 2-bedroom house, 12 square feet for a 3-bedroom house.

A closet should be located where it is needed. To add a closet is to subtract from living space, so it is a trade-off. Where large rooms are

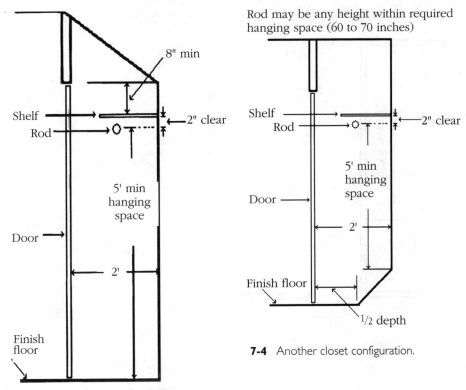

Rod may be any height within required hanging space (60 to 70 inches)

8" min

Shelf

Rod

2" clear

5' min hanging space

Door

2'

Finish floor

7-3 Required closet dimensions.

Shelf

Rod

2" clear

5' min hanging space

Door

2'

Finish floor

¹/₂ depth

7-4 Another closet configuration.

involved, there is space to trade. In homes with small rooms the problem is more serious.

When planning a closet addition to a room, it often works best to use the full wall. The living space otherwise saved is not significant (see FIG. 7-5).

CLOSET COMBINATIONS

Closets often can best be worked in combination in conjunction with an existing wall. In FIG. 7-6, an old farm house is given the modern closet look by combining a coat closet, a bedroom closet and a linen closet using an existing wall.

Figure 7-7 illustrates another combination you can build. Add a parallel wall in the room that can best afford to lose the space. Keep in mind the swing requirement of closet doors when planning closet construction. You don't want doors to take up valuable space because of the wrong swing. In many cases, bifold or sliding doors will solve the problem.

In some older homes, the hall deadends into a bedroom. This can be modified into several different closet combinations. Figure 7-8 shows one

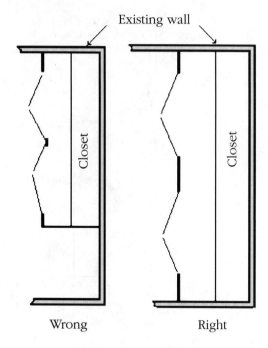

Existing wall

Closet

Closet

Wrong

Right

7-5 Use the full wall.

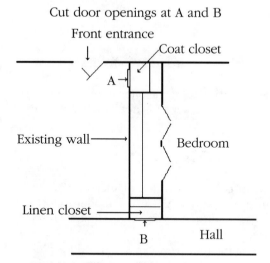

Cut door openings at A and B

Front entrance

Coat closet

A→

Existing wall——→

Bedroom

Linen closet ——→

B Hall

7-6 Building closets in combination.

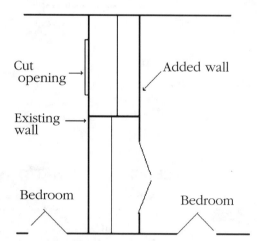

Cut opening→

Added wall

Existing → wall

Bedroom

Bedroom

7-7 Add parallel wall and cut opening in existing wall for two closets.

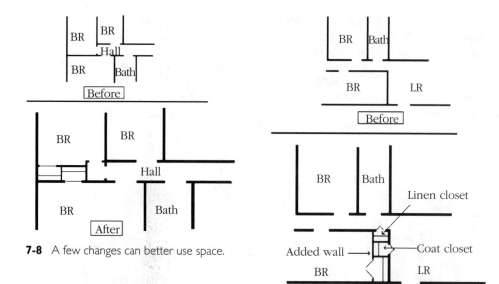

7-8 A few changes can better use space.

7-9 Add a wall and make a combination of three closets.

possibility. Figure 7-9 shows another old house with a typical layout. Use the closet combination approach to solve the problem. Some older homes have a back porch but do not have a bedroom closet or utility room. Figure 7-10 is a design offering a possible solution: a walk-in closet should

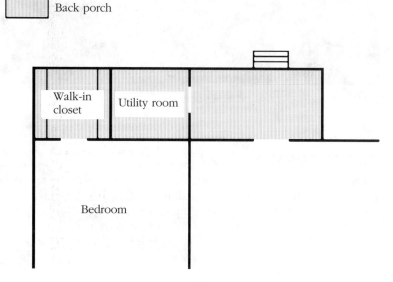

7-10 Converting porch space into closet and utility room.

have a minimum 4-foot depth and a minimum 5-foot width. A 5-foot depth and a width of 6–7 feet is better. Figure 7-11 shows how shelves, hanger bars and storage bins may be arranged.

A stair closet may be an option in some two-story homes (FIG. 7-12). Use care, however, that you do not ruin the open-stair concept that adds to the appearance of the hall, foyer or room. Some architectural designs should not be tampered with.

7-11 A prebuilt unit can end closet clutter.

Milroy Wood Products.

CLOSET CONSTRUCTION

Closet construction includes squaring the closet, installing sole plates, top plates, studs, headers, etc. It is making certain that you have a structural component with which to secure hanging rods and shelves. At the closet ends install a hanging block, as shown in FIG. 7-13.

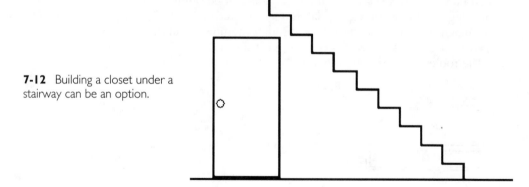

7-12 Building a closet under a stairway can be an option.

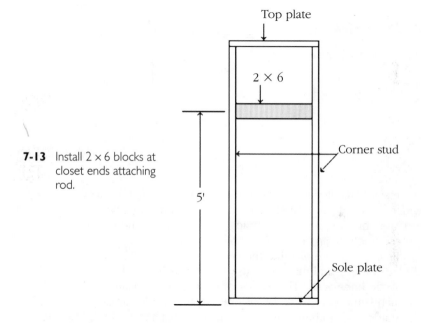

7-13 Install 2 × 6 blocks at closet ends attaching rod.

Top plate

2 × 6

Corner stud

5'

Sole plate

Wall studs Closet wall studs may be 2 × 2s or 2 × 3s to conserve space. You can fit 2 × 4s in the framing by turning the stud sideways. Rip a 2 × 4 down the center for sole and top plates.

Headers Frame closet door header with two 2 × 4s turned edgeways. The header is non-load-bearing and serves only as framing for the opening. When the framing is completed you are ready to apply the inside finish material. Use drywall, plywood or OSB panels, cedar chipboard, or any of the many other materials available, including cedar planks.

Installing rod and shelf Metal rod holders can be screwed directly to the hanging block (or an appropriately located stud) at each end of the closet. Attach the screws to the block through the finish wall. If a shelf is installed over the rod, use a 1 × 6 to support the rod and shelf (see FIG. 7-14). The rod can be removed by lifting it out of the rod slot.

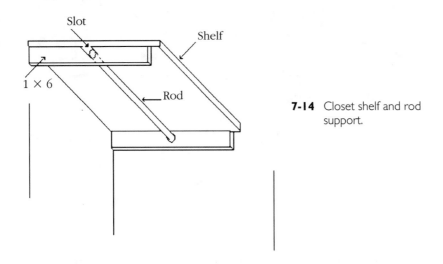

7-14 Closet shelf and rod support.

Install a center brace for the rod and shelf if the closet is 4 feet or wider. A closet rod and shelf often supports a lot of weight. Use a metal rod/shelf bracket. Attach the bracket directly to a stud or hanging block at the center of the span.

Prebuilt closet units like the ones shown in FIGS. 7-1 and 7-11 are available for orderly and maximum use of closet space.

Attic knee-wall This space often provides an area for storage compartments and closets. A 5-foot knee-wall provides ample height to hang many items of clothing. Drawer compartments can be built into the knee-wall in bedroom areas for an additional use of storage space.

Lay out the closet dimensions and install the sole plates and top plates. Since it is necessary to finish only the interior walls of the closet, you can frame the closet corners with two corner posts as shown in FIG. 7-15.

Install studs on 16-inch or 24-inch centers, cutting the top of the studs to fit pitch of rafters. Toenail studs to plates with 8d nails. Use two 2 × 4s on edge for the header of the door opening. Be sure to install a hanger block or stud to anchor the rod. Closet doors may be folding, sliding (pocket or by-pass), flush, panel or louvered. Most standard interior doors are 1⅜ inches thick. Folding or sliding by-pass doors are frequently used for large openings. The louvered door works well for closets because it provides constant ventilation.

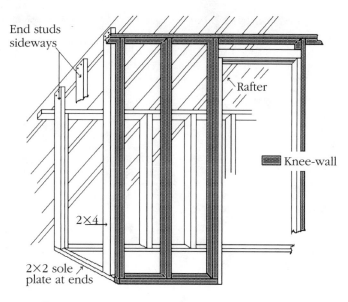

End studs
sideways

Rafter

Knee-wall

2×4

2×2 sole
plate at ends

7-15 Framing the knee-wall closet.

DETERMINING MATERIALS

Materials required depends on the size of the closet and the modifications to the existing structure. A rule of thumb for estimating 8-foot 2 × 4s for plates, studs, headers, etc., required for a closet with members on 24 inches centers is: Closet square feet times 1.75. For example: A closet 2 feet deep and 8 feet wide is:

$$2 \times 8 = 16 \times 1.75 = 28$$

Multiply the closet square feet by 2 to estimate 8-foot 2 × 4s for 16-inch spacing. Estimate wall and ceiling finishing materials on square-foot basis. Compute shelving and hanger rod by linear feet.

ESTIMATING LABOR HOURS

The average do-it-yourselfer should be able to frame an add-on medium-size closet at the rate of one hour per square foot. In the above example of a closet 2 feet deep and 8 feet wide, estimate 16 hours. Large-size closets, such as, walk-ins should take less time per square foot. For example, a 5 × 7 walk-in should require only 22 hours to lay out and frame.

Chapter **8**

Insulation

Insulation manufactured for buildings is designed to slow or reduce heat transfer. Effective insulating materials reduce the flow of heat from the structure during cold periods and restrict the flow into the building during hot periods. Most insulating materials do this by trapping air in the mass of tiny pockets within the material, thereby preventing heat movement in either direction. Another insulating material is the reflective type with foil surfaces that reflect the heat. Foil-covered batts or blankets combine the reflective and air entrapment concepts.

Insulation cuts down on heat transfer through the floors, walls, and ceilings of a structure, which in turn reduces the amount of heating and cooling energy required, lowering operating costs.

Old homes were built without insulation. New homes are required by most building codes to be insulated at specific values.

TYPES OF INSULATION

Most insulation materials are lightweight and produced in the following forms:

- Blanket
- Batt
- Rigidboard
- Reflective
- Loose fill
- Foam

Common thermal insulating materials include mineral fibers (made from glass, rock, and slag), vegetable fibers (such as wood, cane, cotton, and redwood bark), expanded mineral granules (such as vermiculite and perlite), vegetable granules (such as ground cork), foamed materials (glass and synthetic resins like urethane and styrene), and aluminum foil.

Blankets, batts, and rigidboard are made from fibers or granules that are mixed with binders and formed into various widths, lengths, and thicknesses. Blankets and batts come unfaced or faced on one or both sides with a paper with an asphalt content, or with a reflective metal foil that acts as a vapor barrier. You can get blankets or batts in widths to fit between framing members spaced on standard centers. Paper-faced blankets or batts have continuous paper flanges along the long edges for stapling or nailing to studs and joists.

Rigidboard insulation made from foamed materials (both glass and synthetic resins like styrene and urethane), and aluminum foil offer relatively high R-values per inch of thickness.

Reflective insulation is made from reflective foils such as aluminum. It retards the flow of infrared heat passing through air space. The foil surface must face an air space of ¾ inch or more to be effective. Once the reflective surface touches surrounding materials, it is ineffective as a reflective insulator.

Loose fill is poured or blown into place. Glass fiber, and rock wool are two types of loose-fill insulation in common use. The blow application requires blowing machines. Pouring is done by hand. Loose fill is available in bags or bales.

Foam insulation is actually a foam-in-place insulation. It is a two-part synthetic resin material in liquid form that is mixed together and squirted into a cavity. Within a specified time after mixing, a foaming action takes place, filling the cavity.

INSULATION VALUES

The Department of Energy (DOE) and Council of American Building Officials (CABO) have developed thermal (insulation) requirements for the five different climate zones (see FIG. 8-1).

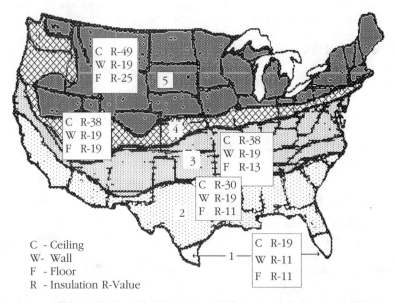

8-1 Insulation requirements by geographic zones.

To get the insulation values recommended in the figure, you may have to use double layers of insulation or combine layers with different R-values. For example, an R-38 added to an R-11 gives a R-49.

If you intend to add batts or blanket insulation over existing attic insulation, unfaced batts are preferable. Unfaced batts prevent moisture from condensing in the existing insulation. If unfaced batts are not available, faced batts can be used if the facing is cut open or torn at frequent intervals to allow free passage of moisture. A 6-inch slash or tear every foot would probably be sufficient.

VAPOR BARRIERS

Many batts and blankets have vapor barriers already attached to one side. Other forms of insulation, such as loose fill, require a separate membrane of polyethylene. Vapor barriers prevent condensation of moisture in insulated spaces. When warm, moisture-laden air comes in contact with a cold surface, droplets of moisture collect on that surface. Insulation is ruined when moisture continually collects within it.

Install the vapor barrier on the warm side (nearest the building interior) of the insulation. The vapor barrier should have a permeability rating of 1 perm or less. (One perm equals one gram of water vapor transmission per square foot, per hour, for each inch of mercury difference in vapor pressure). Plastic sheet (polyethylene) material, coated or laminated paper, and aluminum foil qualify. Ordinary 15- or 30-pound asphalt-saturated felt does not qualify.

It is understandable that the greater the temperature difference from one side of the wall to the other, and the greater the relative humidity of the air on the warm side, the more effective the vapor barrier must be.

INSULATING A BASEMENT

Your basement conversion plan should include insulating the exterior walls. To provide space for batts or rigid insulation board on a masonry wall, apply furring strips to the wall as shown in FIG. 8-2. Use 2 × 2 or 2 × 3 strips. Use a good adhesive to attach the furring strips to the masonry wall.

Install insulation between furring strips, as illustrated in FIG. 8-3. The insulation may be applied using adhesive. Apply a spot of adhesive to each corner and in the middle of the back of the insulation and press into position.

After the insulation is in place you are ready to install the drywall panels. Run a bead of adhesive the length of the furring strip, as shown in FIG. 8-4, and install panels. Follow the adhesive manufacturer's instructions.

Extruded polystyrene rigid panels can also be used over a basement masonry wall. Apply it with a slurry (a soupy mixture of cement, sand and water) of cement mortar. The wall is completed with a plaster finish. Extruded polystyrene has a good resistance to vapor movement, requiring no other vapor barrier.

While we are on the subject of basement insulation and vapor barriers, how can you know whether there is a vapor barrier under the con-

8-2 Installing furring strips to basement masonry wall with adhesives.

8-3 Applying rigidboard insulation between furring strips using adhesive.

8-4 Spreading adhesive to furring strips for paneling installation.

Macco Adhesives.

crete slab floor unless you built the house, wrote the specs, or were present when the floor was poured? An absence of floor moisture does not guarantee the existence of an under-slab vapor barrier. When in doubt, lay a sheet of polyethylene over the slab and put down sleepers. Or, you can put down pressure-treated 1 × 4s directly on the floor, and then lay a sheet of poly film on top of the sleepers. Then nail down a second set of 1 × 4 sleepers on top of the first set. Install the subfloor and finish floor over the sleepers (see FIG. 8-5).

When installing insulation in the basement, don't overlook the area between the floor joists and along stringer joists. This prevents heat loss and the escape of water vapor at the top of the foundation wall. Make sure the vapor barrier faces the interior of the basement and fits tightly against the joists and subfloor.

INSULATING THE ATTIC

Figure 8-6 shows how insulation should provide a blanket around the heated portion of your home. In your attic conversion, insulation must be added to knee-walls, end walls and between the rafters (see FIG. 8-7). Leave any existing attic floor insulation in place. The insulation between

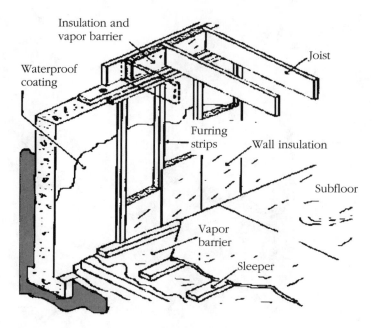

8-5 Basement insulation.

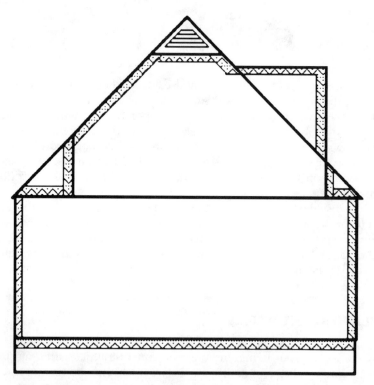

8-6 Enclose the heated portion with insulation.

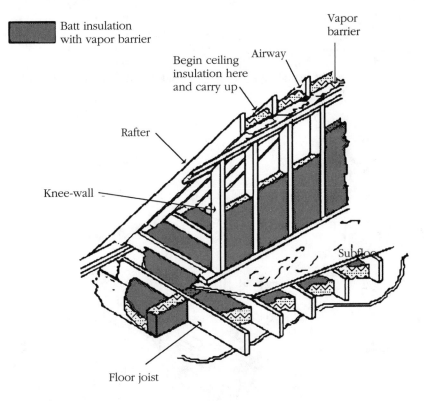

Batt insulation
with vapor barrier

Vapor
barrier

Begin ceiling
insulation here
and carry up

Airway

Rafter

Knee-wall

Subfloor

Floor joist

8-7 Attic knee-wall insulation and vapor barrier.

the rafters should extend upward and over the top of the new ceiling, as seen in FIG. 8-6. Use either blanket or batts with integral vapor barriers.

If there is no insulation in the attic floor, begin insulating the floor by placing batts or blankets between the joists running from the outside wall plate to the knee-wall, the vapor barrier facing down. As seen in FIG. 8-7, the insulation fills the entire joist space directly under the knee-wall. Do not block the airway at the junction of the rafter and top plate.

Next, install batt or blanket insulation between the rafters of the sloping portion of the room, placing the vapor barrier toward the interior of the room. Leave at least a 1-inch airway between the top of the insulation and the roof sheathing, which will allow air to move from behind the knee-wall to the attic area.

If the finish ceiling will extend to the rafter peak (no attic space), then allow for free movement of air between the rafters by installing a ridge vent on the roof. Install batt or blanket insulation in the attic end walls and dormer walls by placing the insulation between the studs and stapling the tabs of the vapor barrier to the studs.

There are two ways to staple the tabs to the studs (and ceiling joists). To minimize vapor loss and reduce condensation, staple the tabs over the edge of the studs as illustrated in FIG. 8-8. This method makes drywall application a little more difficult because it creates an air cushion between the insulation and drywall panels when the panel is first put into position.

The other method is to fasten the tabs to the inner faces of the studs. The method might leave gaps along the edges of the vapor barrier, allowing moisture to escape through these openings.

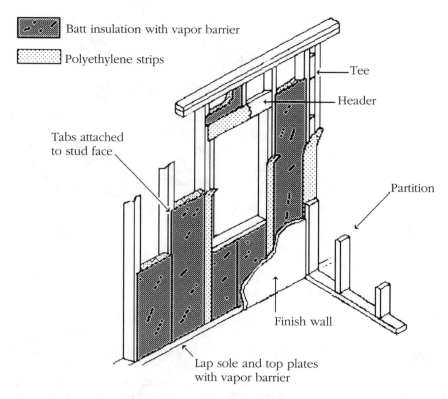

8-8 Installing vapor barrier strips over tees, double studs, and header at openings.

Whenever insulating a wall or ceiling, be sure to place insulation into areas behind electrical boxes, pipes and ducts. Fill the spaces with fitted pieces of batt or loose insulation. Also, pack insulation into spaces between the rough framing and window and door jambs, sills and headers. Staple vapor barrier paper or plastic over tees, double studs and headers at door and window openings.

Enveloping is the installation of a vapor barrier over the interior surface of the entire wall. Install an unfaced friction-type insulation batt without a vapor barrier (FIG. 8-9). The batt is made to fit snugly between framing members spaced 16 or 24 inches o.c. Once the rough-in of duct, plumbing, and wiring is completed, install the insulation and apply vapor barrier over the entire wall, using a minimum 4-mil-thick polyethylene in

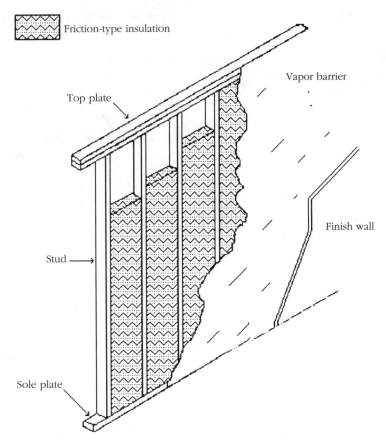

Friction-type insulation

Vapor barrier

Top plate

Finish wall

Stud →

Sole plate

8-9 Enveloping the wall.

8-foot-wide rolls (for 8-foot high ceilings). Completely cover window and door headers, all top and bottom plates, and corners. Do not cut the plastic around window openings until after the finish wall has been installed.

When enveloping, provide a means (such as a slightly opened window) for fresh air movement. A house needs a constant air exchange. (Some experts suggest that some homes and office buildings are built too tightly; that such construction is bad for one's health.)

DETERMINING MATERIALS AND ESTIMATING LABOR HOURS

TABLE 8-1 gives the coverage and installation hours for insulation batts fitting framing spaced 16 or 24 inches o.c. Loose-fill insulation for the attic will take the average do-it-yourselfer one hour to spread 50 square feet 4 inches thick using 9.5 cubic feet of loose fill (6-pound density).

Compute rigid board insulation requirements for basement walls on the basis of number of square feet of wall. Allow two and a half hours to install 100 square feet of 1 inch polystyrene or 2 inches urethane. Glass fiber or mineral fiber boards will take about the same number of hours.

Table 8-1 Batt insulation coverage and labor hours.

Insulation batts		Material		Staples	Labor hours
Size	Square feet	Nr batts per 100 SF	Nr Sq. Ft. for 100 SF wall	Per 100 SF	SF per hour
15 × 24	2.5	40	95	160	65
15 × 48	5.0	20	95	160	70
23 × 24	3.84	26	95	160	75
23 × 48	7.67	13	100	160	80

Notes: Studding and joist space excluded Batts stapled @ 6" o.c.

Chapter 9

Basement conversions

When the typical homeowner looks around for areas to convert into habitable space, he turns to whatever has the most components in place: floor, ceiling, walls, and so on. Why go to the expense and labor of adding a room when there is a basement or attic that can be converted?

Betty and her husband Norman wanted a guest bedroom for out of town guests. Their home is located on a large lot and a room could easily have been added. Instead, they decided to convert the basement into a bedroom (FIG. 9-1) and a game nook.

A water-tight basement can be converted into habitable space. You probably would not want to turn your basement into a living room or

9-1 Basement space converted into guest room.

kitchen because of the limited access, but you can turn the under-used space into a recreation room, office, a hobby and craft room, a studio, or even a study and library away from busy family activities.

When considering a basement bedroom, think also about a bathroom. A bathroom can be added without installing a sewage pumping unit if sewer lines run at or below the basement floor level.

Dampness can be a problem and must be resolved. Condensation at the floor level can also be a problem but it, too, can be eliminated. A basement seepage problem takes on a new and greater meaning when you hope to turn that area into habitable space. A leaking basement will ruin the finish floor coverings as well as damage finish walls, furniture, books, clothes and anything else stored or used in the basement.

CONDENSATION

Condensation is caused when the basement's interior air (which is comparatively warm and humid) meets the cool masonry basement walls, causing water vapor to condense on the wall surface. The word "condensation" means to reduce to a more dense form, i.e., vapor to water.

Condensation occurs when the surface temperature of the wall falls below the dewpoint temperature of the air in the basement. Thus, a rise in relative humidity and temperature, often caused by appliances such as hot water heaters, washers and dryers, can create or add to condensation problems.

Condensation can be minimized by regulating ventilation in the basement. Is there a heating system in the basement? If so, keep basement windows closed when the system is operating. During the spring, until warmer weather has raised the temperature of the ground at the basement walls, keep windows closed. Clothes dryers and gas water heaters release a lot of moisture into the air and should always be vented outside.

The practical solution to basement condensation problems is a vapor barrier. By installing a barrier to vapor between the masonry wall and the basement space, you eliminate the problem. Paint is not a vapor barrier, so painting the walls will not solve the problem. In chapter 8 you learned how to install furring strips and rigid board insulation to masonry walls. This is the solution to condensation in the basement—adding a wall.

Install furring strips, 2 × 2s or 2 × 4s, and cover the furring strips with a vapor barrier. Six-mil polyethylene is a good vapor barrier, as is foam insulation board with a foil vapor barrier. Fit the board between the furring strips and be sure the foil side faces toward the interior of the room. If insulation board has no vapor barrier, install polyethylene over insulation and furring. Finish wall material such as drywall, paneling, or other materials can be secured to the furring strips directly over the vapor barrier.

The water table

The water table is the level of underground water. When it rains, the table rises. In a drought, the table is, of course, lowered. As the table rises the possibility of basement leakage increases. Pressure is applied from underneath and all sides in contact with the water. The water table is higher in some areas than others. Low-lying areas are a bad choice for basements since the water table is higher in such places.

Proceed with caution. The homeowner who has lived in a house for a year or more and has had no problems with basement dampness or seepage can assume that the basement is properly waterproofed. (Do not make this assumption if there has been no appreciable rainfall during the year.)

There are some pretty good sealants on the market, that when applied to the inside of the basement walls might temporarily reduce or stop leaks. This is patch work: it doesn't solve the water problem. Previously, the water seeped into the wall at the weakest seal. Water will continue to saturate the wall and eventually find another inlet into the basement.

A sump pump system can come in several different configurations. It can be installed in a well in the basement floor and be designed to pump water from beneath the basement floor, and also to pump any water that might have leaked into the basement. The water is pumped to a storm sewer drain or natural fall.

A sump pump is essential where there is no storm sewer drain outlet or natural fall to which water from the basement footing drain pipe can be diverted. Such a situation might exist where the basement footing is lower than the surrounding terrain or storm sewer facilities.

A sump pump pulls the water from the footing drain pipe to a higher elevation, where it is diverted away from the area through natural ground flow or to a storm sewer. Figure 9-2 illustrates one possible set-up.

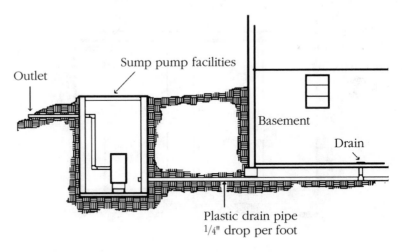

9-2 Using a sump pump to solve basement water problems.

Build the pump housing with concrete block. Pour a concrete floor and lay a basement footing drain pipe to run the water inside the house. The pump is automatically switched on when the water reaches a set level in the pump house. You will want to build the pump house large enough to enter for the purpose of doing maintenance work. Build a strong cover for the house using steel or pressure-treated wood.

Every basement should have a floor drain leading to a natural fall or a storm sewer. The purpose of the drain is to carry off water spilled on the floor, such as can happen when a clothes washer overflows or in the event of a leaking water heater. The floor drain should be installed in a shallow depression, slightly below the top surface of the floor level. A floor drain can prevent serious water damage to the basement and its contents.

BASEMENT CONVERSION REQUIREMENTS

As we've seen, just any basement cannot be converted to habitable space. Before you can plan your conversion you must also consider the natural light (window area), ceiling height, exits, stairs, etc. The codes are specific concerning habitable space, and your local code might have additional requirements.

Ceiling heights of basements without habitable spaces can be as low as 6'8"(6'4" under girders). You'll need a 7'6" ceiling height for habitable space. (Habitable space is a room in a structure used for living, sleeping, eating or cooking. Other areas, such as bathrooms, toilet compartments, closets, halls, storage or utility space and similar areas are not considered habitable space.) A minimum ceiling height of 7'0" is permissible when installing a luminous or drop ceiling (see FIG. 9-3).

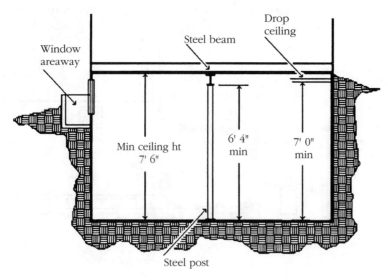

9-3 Minimum basement ceiling heights.

If the girder(s) located in your basement is lower than 6'4" the solution might be to build a partition directly under the girder, making the beam a part of the wall. Most houses have only one girder, which is located mid-way in the house. The girder support posts may also be incorporated into the wall. Support posts do not have to be disguised. They can be left exposed and still be worked into the conversion design, as seen in FIG. 9-4, a basement exercise room equipped with a whirlpool.

Georgia-Pacific.

9-4 Working the design around a basement support post.

Window requirements for a basement change when the basement is turned into habitable space. Natural ventilation is required and may be obtained through an openable window or a year-round mechanical system.

Finished basement spaces used as recreation or similar rooms require natural light glazed area of 8 percent of the floor area. Natural ventilation opening of 4 percent of the floor area is also required. An openable window provides both natural light and ventilation. How can all this work into your plan? A 12 × 12 bedroom has 144 square feet of floor space. The natural light area required, 8 percent of 144, is 11.52 square feet. A 2 × 3 window proves 6 square feet. Two such windows gives you 12 square feet of natural light area, which more than meets the minimum requirement.

The size of the basement window is important. Every room used for sleeping, living, or dining must have two means of egress, at least one of which shall be a door or stairway providing a means of unobstructed travel to the outside at street or ground level.

Each sleeping room, unless it has two doors providing separate ways of escape, or has a door leading outside the building directly, must have at least one outside window that can be opened from the inside without the use of tools, with a sill height not more than 44 inches above the floor, providing not less than 5.7 square feet of openable area and no net clear opening dimension less than 24 inches in height and 20 inches in width. During the planning stage find out what your local building code requires concerning basement conversions.

ADDING A BASEMENT ENTRANCE

A basement with its own outside door makes an ideal conversion project. A sloping lot makes a good building site for a house with a basement with an outside entrance. Ideally, the lot will slope from the rear or end of the house and may be completely clear of any backfill.

What if your basement has no outside door and you must have such an entrance to properly carry out your conversion project? What is the possibility of making a doorway? Look at FIG. 9-5. Begin by excavating the dirt down to the footing. The minimum width of the outside stairway to the basement is 2'8". The minimum tread is 11". The maximum riser is 7½". Figure 9-6 shows the elevation of the plan in FIG. 9-5.

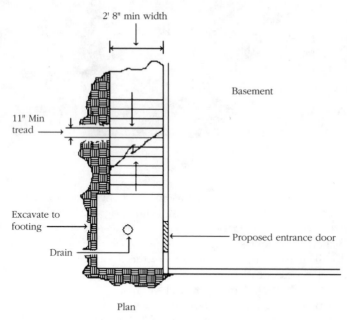

9-5 Excavating for outside entrance.

Entrance doors are 3'0". The landing at the bottom of the stairs should be at least as wide as the door. Three feet is required for the landing and X number of feet for the run of the stairs. Assume the height from the top of the basement floor to finish grade is 7 feet:

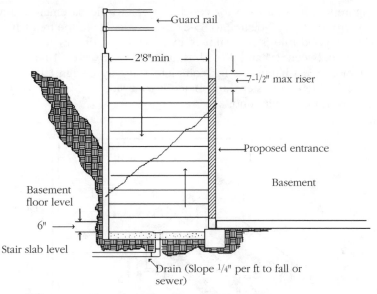

9-6 Stairway construction for outside entrance.

The top of the bottom landing should be a minimum of 6 inches below basement floor level. The finish grade and concrete landing at the top of the stairs will take about 6 inches more, which gives you a stair height of 8 feet from the top of the bottom landing to the top of the top landing (see FIG. 9-7). The 8-foot height will require 13 risers at 7⅜" rise, for a total run of about 11 feet.

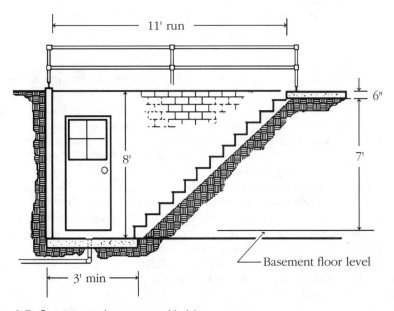

9-7 Basement stairway run and height.

Figure 9-8 shows a form for concrete steps to the basement entrance. Cut the ground to a 30-degree to 35-degree angle. Make the tread 10 inches wide. A good rule is "the sum of two risers and one tread (in inches) should be between 24" and 25". Thus, a 7–7½" riser with a 10–11" tread is acceptable. (See Chapter 12 for complete stairway design.) Use a 2 × 6 along each side of the steps and brace it to a side wall, or brace it with stakes driven into the ground.

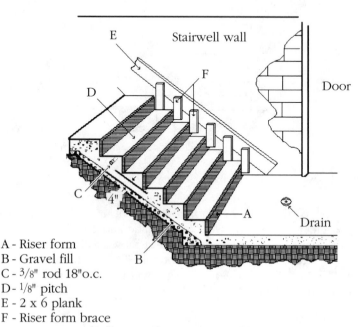

A - Riser form
B - Gravel fill
C - 3/8" rod 18"o.c.
D - 1/8" pitch
E - 2 x 6 plank
F - Riser form brace

9-8 Designing and building concrete basement steps.

If you butt the steps against a side wall, mark the location of the riser and tread on the wall. Nail supports for the riser forms to the 2 × 6 at the marked locations. Make the riser form boards the same width as the height of the riser. Place all riser forms into position and brace them so they'll hold when pouring the concrete. Pitch treads ⅛" downward toward the front to ensure proper drainage—you don't want water standing on the steps or the stairway will be a hazard during the winter.

Place ⅜" reinforcement rods parallel to treads about 18 inches o.c. Pour the steps directly on the ground or on gravel fill. Do not use a wet mix; the concrete must be stiff enough to prevent excess slumping. Work the concrete against the face of the riser forms to obtain a good finish. Give the treads a broom finish to avoid a slippery surface.

Install a drain at the bottom of the steps (FIG. 9-6), using a solid plastic pipe to drain surplus water to a storm sewer, natural fall, or sump pump well. Install an isolation joint where the steps join the building. Use ½-inch-thick asphaltum-impregnated felt. When the concrete has set, remove the forms. Install a handrail for the stairway and a guardrail at the side and rear of the stairwell (FIG. 9-7).

Cutting the doorway

Measure the exact dimensions for the door and jamb materials. Define the position of the door opening, using a level to plumb the cut lines. Mark the top and bottom positions and snap a chalk line through the points. When cutting opening on inside and outside of the wall, make certain the cutting lines line up exactly. Drill through the wall at the top right corner of the opening and measure all cutting lines from that point.

Use a masonry saw to make a neat cut. Because you have marked the cut lines on both inside and outside, a cut on both sides of the wall will cut through most basement walls. Always use protective goggles and face mask when using a masonry cutting blade.

You can cut the doorway using a chisel, but don't try cutting completely through the wall as you proceed. Instead, etch a shallow cut along the cut lines. Repeat the etching on the opposite side. Keep cutting along the lines until there is a complete break through the wall. Remove the masonry and dress the opening.

Follow the same steps when cutting window openings (see FIG. 9-9).

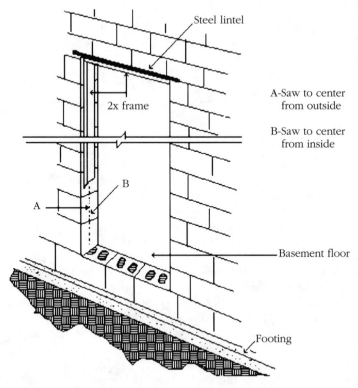

9-9 Cutting basement doorway.

The door opening will not extend to the top of the basement wall. Window openings may extend to the top of the wall. Steel lintels can often be inserted into a slot in the top line to support the wall above the opening during the cutting. Sawing or chiseling often loosens the blocks above the opening. In this case, remove the blocks above the opening, usually in step-fashion as seen in FIG. 9-10.

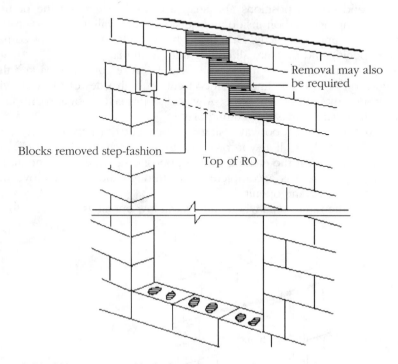

9-10 How to remove blocks from above opening.

Install a steel lintel above the door or window opening. The lintel must be wider than the opening. If it falls at a mortar joint, rake out the mortar joints at each side and slide the lintel into position. Do not rake out more mortar from the joint than is required to fit the lintel. If the lintel's position does not fall at a mortar joint, saw or chisel a notch in the masonry in which to position the lintel. Make the notch large enough to allow a half-inch mortar joint above and below the lintel. Install the lintel and replace any blocks that were removed from above the opening (see FIG. 9-11).

In most houses there is a 2 × 8 sill plate. A joist header is commonly used on the sidewalls. The end walls also have a 2 × 8 sill plate and a joist stringer. Except in hip roof construction, the end walls do not support roof weight.

The need for temporary supports depend on the location of the opening. Where the sill plate or the joist header is continuous over the opening, temporary supports are not needed for openings under 4 feet on a

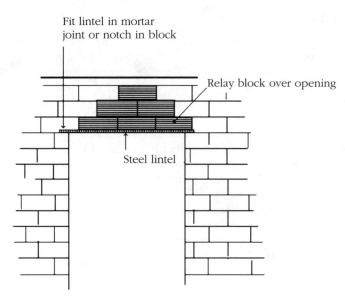

Fit lintel in mortar joint or notch in block

Relay block over opening

Steel lintel

9-11 After installing steel lintel in door opening, relay block over opening.

one-story house. To be on the safe side, erect temporary support as shown in FIG. 9-12 for openings over 4 feet, and on a two-story house. Space doubled 2 × 4 posts 24" o.c. Use a 2 × 4 top plate and a 2 × 4 or larger member as a bottom plate for the supports.

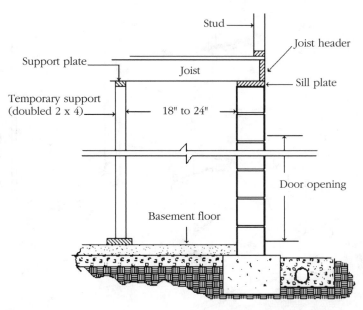

Stud

Joist header

Support plate

Joist

Sill plate

Temporary support (doubled 2 x 4)

18" to 24"

Door opening

Basement floor

9-12 Install temporary support for floor when cutting openings in basement wall.

Framing the door opening

For durability, use pressure-treated wood 2 inches nominal thickness to frame openings in a basement wall. Anchor the framing members securely. To construct the door frame lay the three pieces out on the floor and nail the side members to the top piece with three 16d nails. Wood screws may be used in lieu of nails. Pre-drill holes through the side members when using screws, and use three screws long enough to extend through the side members and into the top piece at least 1½ inches.

Use anchor screws with lead shields to secure the side members to the masonry. Drill holes in the masonry, and insert the lead shields in the holes, keeping the shield flush with the masonry surface. Line up the shields with their corresponding positions on the frame members, mark the location on the frame member, and drill holes for the screws. Use a minimum of three screws for each side, as shown in FIG. 9-13. Use 2-by framing members of sufficient width to allow using molding on the outside, and to flush with the surface of the interior finish wall (see FIG. 9-14).

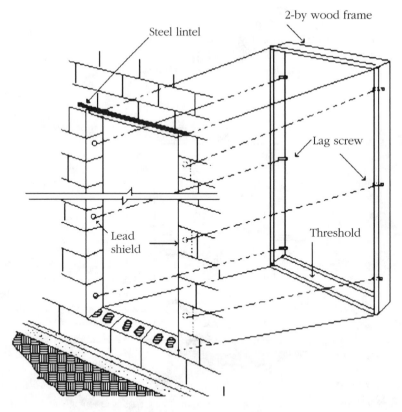

9-13 Securing the door frame with lag screws.

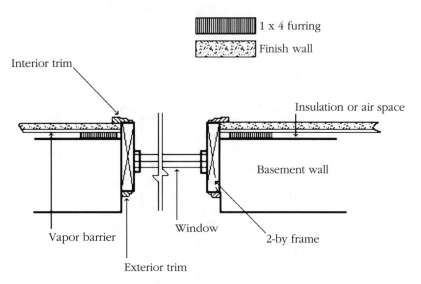

9-14 Framing and trim-out details for basement window.

Framing the window opening

What style window will you install? Metal casement? Double hung? The framing of the opening depends on the window. Keep in mind that where there is a basement outside door as well as a stairway and door to the first floor, a window does not have to be the type that permits a person's exit. The construction of the window sill depends on the type of windows you have selected for your conversion. A double-hung window comes with a sill sloped to shed water (see FIG. 9-15). Certain styles of windows require a masonry sill to divert water (see FIG. 9-16). Allow for such sills in the planning stage and measure the opening accordingly. The size of the opening height must allow for the thickness of the masonry sill and the top and bottom wood members of the frame. Caulk all joints between the frame and masonry, using a quality flexible latex caulking compound.

Cut the opening to allow for a 4-inch-minimum thickness of the masonry sill and the thickness of the 2-by wood framing members. Measure the required length of the rough opening from the lintel down to the top of the masonry sill. Measure both sides of the opening, marking the point at the sill top.

When you pour the concrete mix to form the sill, it is not necessary to fill all the cells of the concrete block below the sill. Do this: Place metal screen or building paper six or seven inches down inside the cells of the top layer of block. Place form boards at the position you marked on both sides of the opening for the masonry sill. Build the form to allow a minimum one-inch projection beyond the outside wall. Use clamps to secure the form boards to the wall, as illustrated in FIG. 9-17. Brace the form from below.

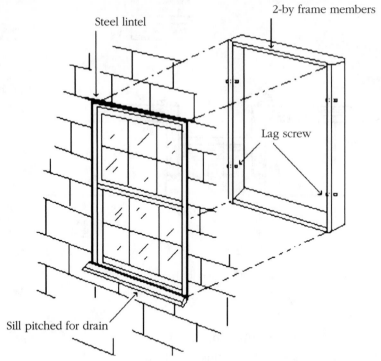

9-15 Framing and installing the double-hung window.

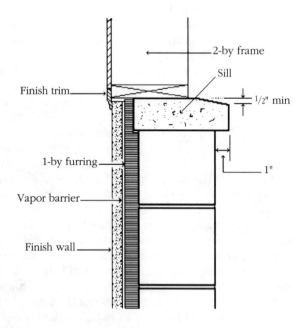

9-16 Installing masonry window sill.

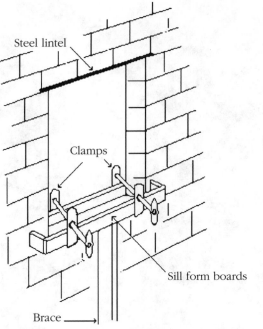

Steel lintel

Clamps

9-17 Clamping the sill form boards into place.

Sill form boards

Brace

Fill the form with a concrete mix not too wet. You want the mix just wet enough to work smoothly. Slope the fill for a ½ inch drop to the front edge. Use a trowel to work the sill smooth.

DESIGNING THE BASEMENT CONVERSION

Do you want space in which the family can spread out; a room in which to entertain and where recreation can take on many forms? Look at FIG. 9-18. Or is it a bathroom and bedroom your growing family needs? Look at FIG. 9-19; the bedroom has its own built-in furniture for study and storage. Figure 9-20 illustrates that basement baths can be as modern and stylish as any first floor bath. Or was it a home office you had in mind for your conversion? Look at FIG. 9-21; with a little imagination and some careful planning your basement project can be a showplace.

Don't think that basement conversion can't be a challenge. There may be some difficult obstacles to work around and you have to use your imagination to make the obstacle appear a part of the design. The existing windows may be small and located high in the basement wall, the top meeting the bottom of the sill plate. Metal ductwork may be suspended from the floor joists and may appear to be an insurmountable problem.

The interior basement stairway may be the biggest design problem. While you can relocate the stairs, you cannot move the landing because to do so means changing the location of the door leading to the basement from the main floor, which cannot always be done. Figure 9-22 shows a basement with the stairs located at an end wall. You want to convert the open basement into a recreation room with a half bath, and enclose the

Georgia-Pacific.

9-18 With imagination and planning, a basement can be anything you want it to be.

Quaker Maid.

9-19 A basement bedroom can be the perfect solution for a growing family.

Casement windows used
in pairs can brighten
any large room.

Pella/Rolscreen

Opening up the attic with
a glass "dormer."

Pella/Rolscreen

Transform a drab room
into elegant space with
a new wall of windows
and a new treatment
for a high ceiling.

Pella/Rolscreen

Georgia-Pacific

A basement conversion can be anything you want it to be.

Georgia-Pacific

Turning the attic into a quiet retreat is possible with careful planning and hard work.

Pella/Rolscreen

Creating a luxurious bath might be as simple as adding windows to a long wall in a seldom-used bedroom.

Extending a basement conversion into the light of day with an outside entrance under glass.

Pella/Rolscreen

Planning an attic conversion can be a playground for an active imagination. A large window area in the gable can bring an oasis into a small attic room.

Pella/Rolscreen

A suspended ceiling is used to lower a high ceiling in this remodeled farm house.

Georgia-Pacific

Give your enlarged space plenty of natural light for an airy and spacious feel.

When relocating walls or redesigning, consider adding a small office.

The partition between a tiny kitchen and an odd-shaped storage room is removed for new kitchen/dining space.

9-20 Need an extra bathroom? Go down to the basement and design the perfect setting for your family.

Kemper Div., WCI, Inc.

Georgia-Pacific.

9-21 Turning wasted basement space into an office.

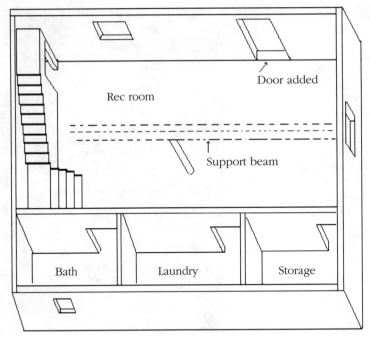

9-22 Basement conversion design.

washer and dryer in a separate room. An outside entrance to the basement is also in your plans.

You can also convert a similar basement into an office/study. Your need may be book shelves and computer, printer, and copier space. Your spouse want a music room in which to train piano students. You might come up with a plan like that in FIG. 9-23. But there's a problem. The stairs are located in the center of the basement and not at an end wall. In such an event you would work out a floor plan similar to FIG. 9-24. Figure 9-25 illustrates how a basement might be converted into bedroom space and a bathroom.

The basement stairway can present a problem because of the space it requires. If an outside entrance to the basement exists, or if you're adding one, replace the standard stairway with a spiral staircase if it will give the space needed.

If your basement is below the sewer line running from your house it will be necessary to install mechanical equipment (pump) to lift the waste to the sewer line. You might want a plumber's bid for the pump and installation charges early in the planning stage.

Installing the subflooring

As we have already seen, a subfloor can be applied directly on sleepers (see Chapter 5). As a reminder, ½" plywood or ⁷⁄₁₆" OSB panels make a good base for ⅜" particle board. Lay the panels so the edges and ends do

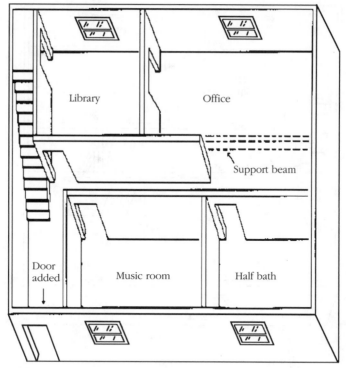

9-23 A basement conversion designed for varied activities.

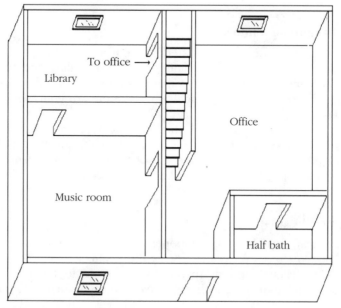

9-24 Designing a basement conversion with stairs in center.

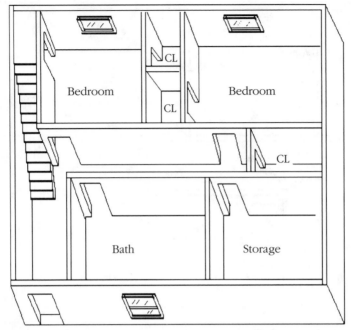

9-25 A conversion design for a growing family.

not match the edges and ends of the subfloor. Space the panels in accordance with the manufacturer's recommendations.

Boxing basement windows

Most basement windows are located as high as possible in the wall, leaving little, if any, space for installing the finish ceiling and trim. The solution is to build a three-sided valance around the window using ¼-inch-thick plywood for the top and 1 × 6 white pine or equivalent for the three sides.

Make the valance long enough to allow space for open drapes. About 9 inches to each side of the window is usually sufficient for the drapes. Figure 9-26 shows how to attach the top of the completed valence to the bottom of the ceiling joists. Wall molding is installed at the level desired.

Boxing iron beams

Steel girders are load-bearing components that should not be disturbed. Install wooden lattices on both sides of the beam. Use 1 × 2-inch strips and 1 × 3-inch center supports spaced 16 inches o.c. to support each lattice. Nail the lattices to 1 × 2-inch cleats fixed on each side of the beam, as illustrated in FIG. 9-27.

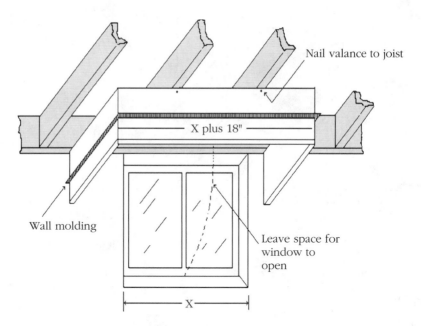

9-26 Install a three-sided valance around basement window.

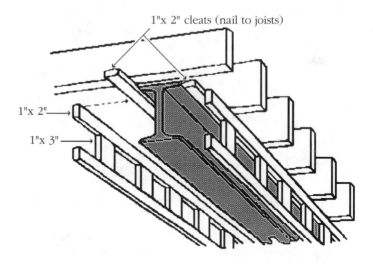

9-27 Make lattice same width and length as steel beam, one to each side of beam.

Enclose the beam by applying a finish material to each lattice. A finish that matches the walls or a wall works quite well. Attach corner moldings as shown in FIG. 9-28. If your basement has air ducts running parallel to the girder, enclose both the girder and duct, as shown in FIG. 9-29.

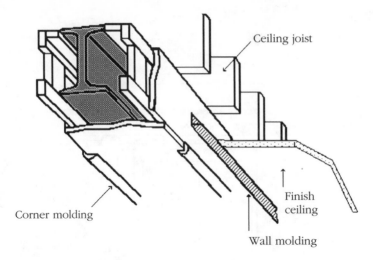

Ceiling joist

Finish
ceiling

Corner molding

Wall molding

9-28 Enclosed beam can be an attractive feature of a conversion.

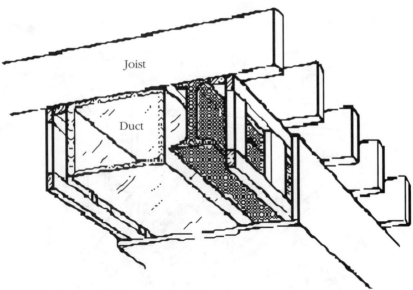

Joist

Duct

9-29 The beam and duct can be boxed together.

Boxing around basement stairways

Nail 1 × 3-inch cleats into the ceiling joists. The distance from the old ceiling (if there is one) to the new ceiling will determine the width of the valance material. Use 1 × 4-inch or 1 × 6-inch white pine. Nail the valance to the cleats. Cover the seam with standard molding. Install the wall molding at the desired height, as seen in FIG. 9-30.

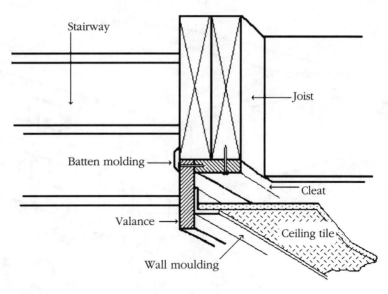

Stairway

Joist

Batten molding

Cleat

Valance

Ceiling tile

Wall moulding

9-30 Stairway finishing details.

If you convert basement space to a bedroom it is considered a habitable room for year-round occupancy. If you convert basement space to a recreation room, bathroom, den or utility room, it is not considered habitable space for year-round occupancy. When the conversion is for year-round occupancy, the basement floor can be no more than 48 inches below the exterior ground level. Figure 9-31 illustrates this requirement: Here's the formula:

$$\frac{\text{Area of earth against the hab. wall (sq. ft.)}}{\text{Length of hab. wall (lin. ft)}} = 4 \text{ ft. max.}$$

Your computation for FIG. 9-32 looks like this:

$$\frac{\dfrac{(6'+3' \times 16)}{2} + \dfrac{(3'+0 \times 10)}{2}}{16' \times 12'} = \frac{72+15}{28} = 3.10 \text{ ft. average}$$

Figure 9-32 shows how your basement bedroom might look.

ESTIMATING YOUR LABOR HOURS

Any estimate of labor involving basement conversion work can only be a ball park figure, particularly where cutting openings in masonry walls are concerned.

Excavating

In most cases, you will excavate by hand. Heavy equipment working close to a basement wall can cause damage to the wall.

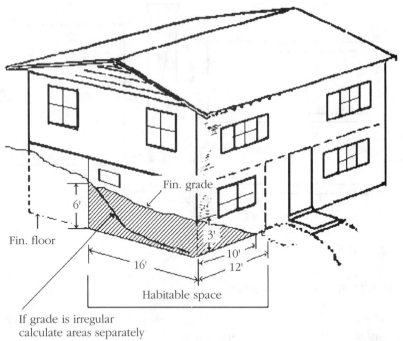

Fin. grade

6'

Fin. floor

3'

16'   10'
       12'

Habitable space

If grade is irregular
calculate areas separately

9-31 Finish grade restrictions.

Quaker Maid.

9-32 A basement bedroom can be spacious and cheerful.

Estimate the trench (for drain pipes) at their actual size plus one foot for working room. For walls that will be given a waterproofing treatment, allow about 32 inches for working room. You will need about the same space for cutting window and door openings. TABLE 9-1 provides hours per cubic yard when digging by hand.

Table 9-1   Hours per cubic yard of hand excavation.

	Trench Depth in Feet			
Soil Type	3	5	8	10
Light	.7	.75	.85	.9
Medium	.85	.9	.9	1.0
Heavy	1.1	1.10	1.25	1.3
Hard pan	1.3	1.4	1.6	1.7

The amount of trench a man can excavate depends on the kind of dirt, how high he must lift the dirt, the extent of pick digging required, and the weather conditions. A pick is generally required for loosening the soil and lifting is accomplished with a round-pointed, long-handled shovel. It takes about 150 to 200 shovels of dirt to excavate a cubic yard under normal conditions. If the dirt is not to be used as fill, hours will be needed to spread the loose dirt over the yard or hauled away.

Cutting openings

How long does it take a skilled craftsman to cut openings in a concrete block wall? Look at TABLE 9-2. You might want to double or triple these estimates for your project.

Table 9-2   Skilled labor hours required to cut openings in concrete block wall.

Wall Thickness	Manhours per Linear Foot
8 inches	0.25
10 inches	0.35
12 inches	0.50

Other labor

Allow four hours to install a wooden door frame for a 3'0" × 6'8" door in basement wall opening and three hours for a 3 × 4 window. Estimate four and a half hours to install a solid core, exterior door, and three hours to install the window. Hours include installing door threshold and exterior trim.

You will need about four hours to build a form for a masonry window sill and pour the concrete. Basement boxing work is tedious work, and you want to take the time to do it right. Estimate lattice and boxing at 10 hours per 25 linear feet.

Masonry walls may be painted. For unpainted interiors of block basement walls, use a primer compatible with the finish coat. You can use a latex block filler as first coat or a latex primer and finish with a latex house paint.

When repainting, scrape clean surfaces that are scaling, peeling or starting to chalk—a wire brush will do the job. Fill any cracks with a patching compound. Remove all cracked and loose caulking. Use a latex primer as first coat and latex house paint for finish coat. You can brush or roll on the primer and finish coat.

The typical do-it-yourselfer can comfortably brush wall paint on a masonry surface at the rate of 500 square feet in 8 hours. Allow about four hours to roll on 500 square feet. Add extra time for tedius trim work such as cutting in different colors for the wall and ceiling.

Chapter **10**

Attic conversions

Attic conversion, as with basement conversion, is vertical expansion. The cost to expand vertically can be less than a third that of adding a room from the ground up. The more of the work you do, the more you save. The attic can become almost anything you want it to be. How about a private world for that athletic and growing boy? See (FIG. 10-1.). Or, you could turn the space into a office, see (FIG. 10-2). A study might be well-used by your college-bound teenager (FIG. 10-3). The attic bathroom can also be a show place. Your design might look something like FIG. 10-4.

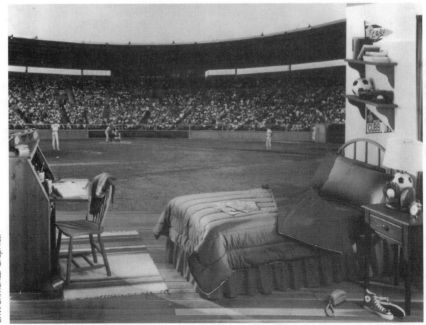

Environmental Graphics.

10-1 An attic bedroom can extend beyond four walls.

10-2. Turning attic space into office space.

Quaker Maid.

10-3. An attic corner becomes a quiet study area.

Milroy Wood Products.

10-4. An attic bath does not have to be cramped.

LOOK BEFORE YOU LEAP

When was the last time you bought 12-foot 2 × 8s? You and yours could go out to a fine salad bar and pig out for what you'd have to pay for a couple. The cost of building materials should make any do-it-yourself project a carefully thought-out plan. Mistakes can be terribly expensive.

If your home is one of those old houses with a high attic, the conversion possibilities are many. Most such houses were stick-built in the conventional manner and can be readily converted. A truss roof, however, can be a problem if removing some of the components is required. Consult a professional builder before removing any part of a truss roof. In most instances, few, if any, members can be removed.

Attics with insufficient roof heights cannot be converted. Figure 4-2, Chapter 4, illustrates height requirements for a convertible attic. The height under the peak of the roof should be 7 feet 6 inches. As a general rule of thumb, the rise of the roof should be a third or half its span. (Span is the distance from outside wall plate to opposite outside wall plate.) A house width of 24 feet and a ⅓ roof rise would have an 8-foot attic ceiling at the peak. The steeper the roof pitch, the more usable floor area available. Knee walls should be 4–5 feet high.

Attics with insufficient floor support cannot be converted without reinforcing the framing. Most houses were built with 2 × 6 ceiling joists. While 2 × 6s are adequate in conventional ceiling construction, they are hardly sufficient to support the floor weight of a habitable attic. Additional floor joists will have to be installed.

You can turn an attic into habitable space provided there is sufficient ceiling height and floor support. While roofs can be redone to gain additional height, few homeowners will want to undergo such expense. You can, however, install the additional floor joists needed to provide adequate floor support.

Is there a stairway to the attic? Your attic may have a narrow stair or a retractable stair, neither of which is adequate for a converted attic. While planning the project locate on your attic floor plan a 3 × 13-foot space at a 30- to 35-degree angle for the stairs. Determine what must be done on the floor below to accommodate the stairway. Consider also the possibility of using a spiral stairway that can be squeezed into a 5-foot diameter space. An outside stairway may also be an option.

An attic with a bedroom and no outside stairway must have windows of sufficient size and configuration to qualify as egress windows.

An attic might obtain heat from the floor below through an open stairway or open floor vents. This is overflow air and should not be the sole source of heat because it is not always sufficient or controllable. Your present central system may not be large enough to handle the extra load.

FLOOR JOIST

The span of the floor joist determines the size stock to use. Not all wood species have the same structural strength and different grades within the same specie makes a difference in the allowable span. No. 2 southern pine in the 2 × 8 size can, when spaced 16 inches o.c., easily handle spans up to 12 feet. So can Ponderosa pine, western hemlock, lodgepole pine and some other species, based on calculations of 40 pounds per square foot uniform live load.

In the attic, ceiling height is critical, and to add a wider member (as when installing 2 × 8s to reinforce a 2 × 6 floor system) will cut a couple inches off the ceiling height. For a 2 × 6 joist system in most attics you can add 2 × 6s to strengthen the floor, as shown in FIG. 10-5, assuming it is constructed in the conventional manner, illustrated in FIG. 10-6. Figure 10-7 shows truss construction; you can see how a truss-built roof system does not readily lend itself to being tampered with. In FIG. 10-6 the diagonal, or trough, braces can be removed after the knee wall is constructed. Wider joist members may be used in conjunction with 2 × 4 or 2 × 6 attic floor system provided the ceiling height permits.

Floored attics are nice unless it is one in which the floor system must be reinforced before it can be converted. Use care when removing the flooring because it is material that can be used as the subfloor. You may also have to remove the braces and trough shown in FIG. 10-6. Install temporary bracing to maintain the rafters at their present set position until the knee walls have been constructed. Cut the ends of all joists at an angle to fit between the roof sheathing and bear fully on the top plate.

When installing the added joist against an existing joist, stagger 10d or larger nails 16 inches o.c. along the span. The narrow space between the roof sheathing and the top plate is seldom large enough to give you room

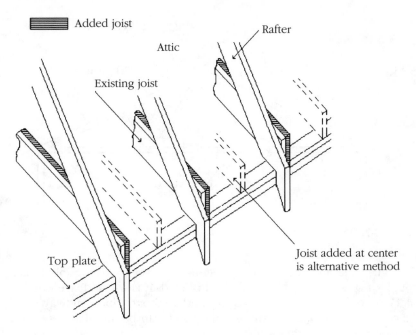

10-5. Reinforce attic floor by adding same-size joists.

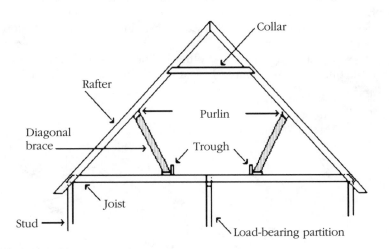

10-6. A conventionally framed attic.

to toenail the joist to the top plate. You can, however, toenail the added joist to the top plate of any load-bearing wall (use two 8d nails).

Use care when nailing to existing joists so as not to damage the ceiling underneath. Excessive hammering can loosen drywall at nail heads. Bracing the existing joist firmly with your foot while nailing helps reduce vibration.

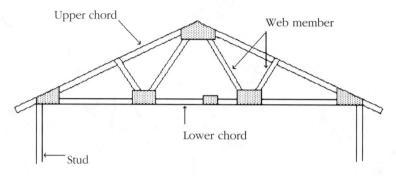

10-7. W-type light wood truss.

When the added joists are positioned between existing joists, nail in the 2 × 4 or same size blocking, as illustrated in FIG. 10-8. Place one block as close to the side walls as possible and a second block midway the distance to the load-bearing wall. A third block can be installed between the joists at the load-bearing wall.

Replace any insulation you disturb. If there is no insulation, now is the time to add it. Install the insulation from outside top plate to outside top plate. Leave space for air to move from the soffit vents up between the rafters to the peak of the roof. Insulation reduces heat transmission to and from the rooms below.

How will you get the joist and other building materials into the attic? Now is the time to think about it. Few attic stairs are arranged so a 12-foot

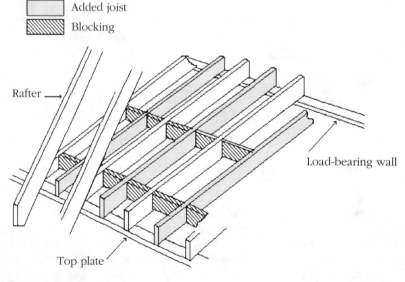

10-8. Using blocking to strengthen floor system.

2 × 8 or a 4 × 8 panel can be brought through the front door, down the hall, and up to the attic. If you're building a dormer or cutting a hole in the gable end for an outside entrance or a window, then getting material to the attic is no problem. Make sure you consider this potential problem during the planning stage.

Electrical wires

Most attics are not wired except for a pull-chain light or a couple lights and a switch, so electrical wires above the floor are rarely a problem. Wires to light fixtures in the ceiling below might run over the top of the attic floor joist in unfloored attics. You'll have to relocate any existing wires before beginning to work. If the joists are furred, run the wire between the ceiling and the joists, as shown in FIG. 10-9. Run the wire through holes drilled in the center of joists or along the joists when the ceiling is nailed directly to the joists.

Subfloor

Once you have marked the area to be cut out for the stairway, you are ready to secure the subfloor. Use ½ -inch plywood, ⁷⁄₁₆ -inch OSB panels, or the old flooring material you removed. Butt the subflooring against the

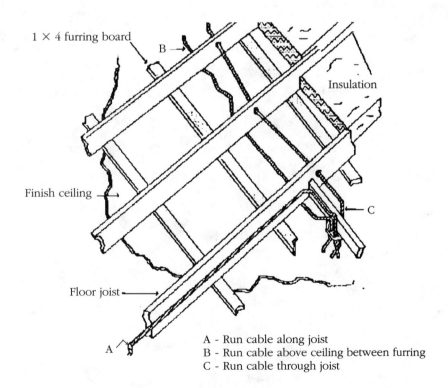

1 × 4 furring board
B →
Insulation
Finish ceiling
C
Floor joist
A
A - Run cable along joist
B - Run cable above ceiling between furring
C - Run cable through joist

10-9. Reroute electrical cable under attic floor.

rafter and floor joist juncture at the eave to minimize gaps. (The area behind the knee wall is usable storage space and should be completely subfloored.) When installing the underlayment on top of subfloor panels remember to stagger the ends at least the distance of two joists to give the floor additional stability.

INSTALLING KNEE WALLS

While the knee wall cannot be in the same place as the diagonal brace, the wall will serve to support the roof. In attics the knee wall height can be as low as 4 feet. However, the recommended practice is to partition off any space having less than a 5-foot ceiling height.

Do this: snap a chalk line for the knee wall sole plate position. The 2 × 4 sole plate will run perpendicular to the run of the joists except that in the end walls of some hip roofs and a few other instances, the sole plate might run parallel to the run of several joists. Secure the plate to each perpendicular joist with 12d or 16d nails.

Look at FIG. 10-10: this is how to install the knee wall top plate and nailers. Cut the studs to fit the angle formed by the top plate. The cut will be the same as the rafter pitch. Position the studs to fall directly under the rafters. The finish ceiling treatment you use will determine the location of the nailing ledger. In hip roof construction, the knee wall is carried around all four walls (see FIG. 10-14).

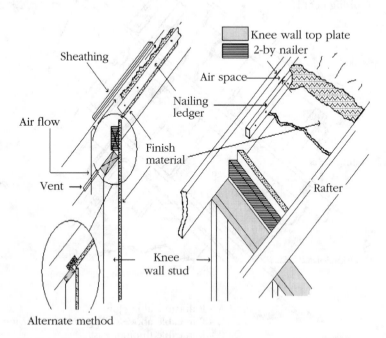

10-10. Using a nailer at knee wall top plate.

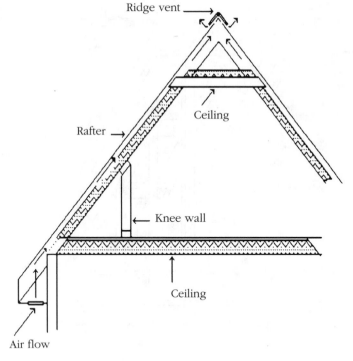

Ridge vent

Ceiling

Rafter

Knee wall

Ceiling

Air flow

10-11. Air flow requires a minimum of 1 inch clearance.

Insulate the knee wall as shown in FIG. 8-7, Chapter 8. Make certain a minimum 1-inch air space is maintained at all points (see FIG. 10-11).

Most rafters used in homes are 2 × 6s, so rafter depth must be increased if 6-inch-thick insulation is to be used between the rafters. To increase rafter depth, install 2 × 2 strips along the underside of the rafters using 12d nails or 2½-inch hardened screws spaced 16 inches o.c. (see FIG. 10-14). The greater rafter depth provides sufficient air passage between the top of the insulation and the bottom of the roof sheathing, which allows free air movement and lets built-up hot air escape. A 1-inch minimum airspace is needed. Without adequate air space, heat builds up in the insulation, causing roof shingles to deteriorate faster than normal. Also, condensation can develop between the sheathing and the insulation with changes in temperature.

Attic partition walls that extend to the rafters can be nailed directly to the rafter. A partition wall located between rafter runs might be installed as shown in FIG. 10-12.

Install 2 × 4 blocking between the rafters 24 inches o.c. Secure the blocking in place with 16d nails through the rafter. Nail the 2 × 4 top plate to the blocking using 12d or larger nails. Cut the studs to fit the angle. It is good practice to double the floor joist directly under the partition wall sole plate. Space studs for partition walls at 16 or 24 inches o.c.

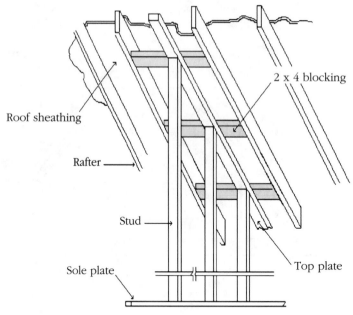

10-12. Install blocking between rafters to secure partition wall.

INSTALLING RAFTER COLLAR BEAMS

Rafter collar beams are essential components for maintaining roof structural strength. The beam may be 1 × 6 planks, 2 × 4s or 2 × 6s. Collar beams secure rafters together, preventing rafter spread. Not all houses are constructed alike; you might find collar beams installed high or low compared to the height of the attic and pitch of the roof. Also, all the beams may not be identically positioned at the same height or a beam might not be level.

You can make minor adjustments in collar beams. If the beams are too low, they can be moved to a higher position for a higher ceiling. If the collars are not evenly installed, correct the problem by relocating the beams so all will be the same. When repositioning the collar beams, do not remove them all. Redo a couple at the time, working from one end of the attic to the other.

Collar beams can be used as ceiling joists for the attic and, thus, create an air space or attic above the ceiling. If the beams are 1 × 6 planks, replace them with 2 × 4s or larger members, depending on the span. For collar beam spans greater than 6 feet use a 2 × 6 (see FIG. 10-13).

Some hip roofs do not have collar beams. The knee wall in a hip roof is, as stated earlier, carried around the four walls (FIG. 10-14). In a gable roof, the knee wall is limited to two walls.

Vent and insulate the new attic that is created when the finish ceiling is installed on the collar beams. In a hip roof it will be necessary to cut through the shingles and sheathing at the ridge and install a ridge vent. Twelve-inch-

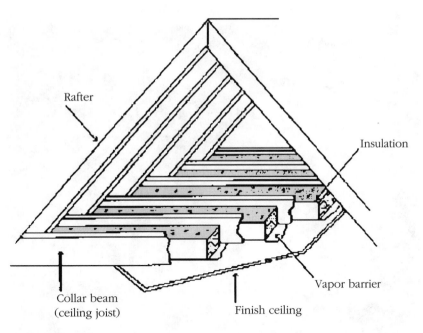

10-13. Creating attic space above the conversion.

thick fiberglass will give the required R-value (R-38) for most areas. Install the vapor barrier side of the insulation facing down, toward the room.

The small attic above the new attic ceiling should have a free ventilating area of $\frac{1}{300}$ or greater of the horizontal area—that is, you'll need one foot of free area for each 300 square feet of attic space. Screen ventilators are recommended. The screen wire takes up a portion of the free ventilating area of a vent as well as the louvers, so select the vent size accordingly. Some vents contain a stamp or label specifying the free ventilating area.

The good thing about collar beams is that you don't have to cover them. Exposed collars can be a part of your design whether it is a vaulted or cathedral ceiling. Where rafters are spaced 16 inches o.c., collar beams are commonly installed on every third rafter. Such spacing is ideal for an exposed-beam design, because it avoids the "crowded beam" look. Figure 10-15 illustrates one possibility for your design.

Exposed collar beams present a massive look when boxed. Use blocks or shims spaced 16 inches o.c. along the beam to furr out the boxing to increase the beam size. A better method might be to add a same-size 2-by on the opposite side of the rafter and box as shown in FIG. 10-16. This increases collar strength. You can further strength the structure by bolting the collar to the rafter using two $\frac{3}{16}$-inch bolts.

Tack the added collar member to the rafter. Drill $\frac{3}{16}$ inch holes through the collar member, the rafter and the opposite collar member. Insert the bolts (with washers) and tighten the nuts. Give the beams a natural, stained, or painted finish. You can, of course, dispense with the boxing, leaving the double collar exposed.

10-14. Rafter depth in this hip roof increased to accommodate 6-inch-thick insulation.

OTHER CONSIDERATIONS

A chimney passing through the attic can be an obstacle to your conversion plan, but just because it is there does not mean you can tap into it and use it as a flu unless there is an extra flu in the chimney, which is not likely.

Have you tried working the chimney into the design as a separator? If you enclose the chimney, be sure to provide a minimum 2 inch clearance between the masonry and framing and all other materials as prescribed by code. Try making the chimney a part of a partition wall (see FIGS. 10-17 and 10-18).

Vent pipes and ducts

A vent (soil) pipe or duct in the attic can be incorporated into a wall or closet or be relocated. If a bathroom is in your design, try locating it where there is easy access to the vent pipe. You might even locate a bathroom wall to enclose the pipe.

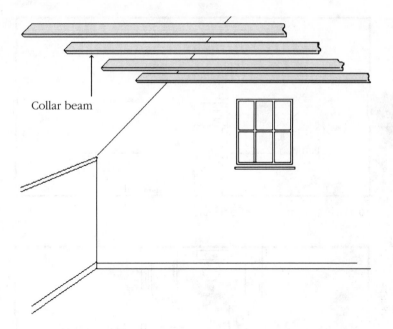

Collar beam

10-15. Designing for exposed collar beams.

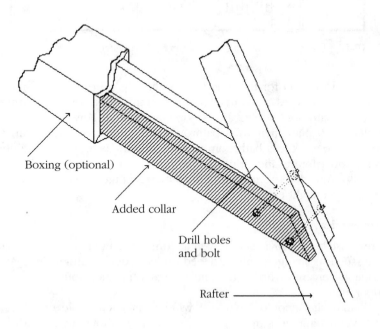

Boxing (optional)

Added collar

Drill holes
and bolt

Rafter

10-16. Selecting the right collar treatment.

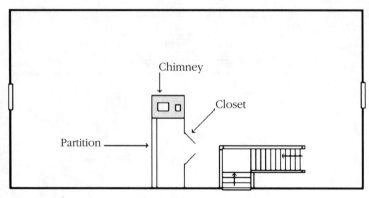

10-17. Making the best of a chimney's location.

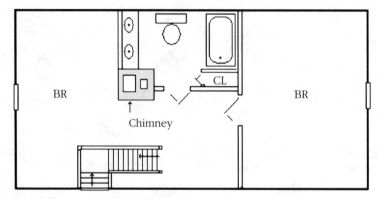

10-18. Designing around a chimney can be a challenge.

A good location for the attic bath is directly over a lower floor bath, permitting easy access to water lines and drains. Take the opportunity to design the bathroom you've always dreamed about. Few people ever get the chance to plan their own bathroom. Let your imagination run wild. Anything can work in a bathroom as long as it all fits together. Use unique windows to capture and bring into a small area the large outdoors (see FIG. 10-19). And don't forget about bathroom storage space. Figure 10-20 is one idea you might use.

Attic windows

There must be a provision for ventilation and natural light. A habitable space, such as living rooms and bedrooms, require natural light (glazed area) as 8 percent of floor area and natural ventilation must be 4 percent of floor area.

Your design should include a window at each gable end (see FIG. 10-22). Ventilating air is moving air, and for air to move, there must be an inlet and an outlet or two openings. In hip roofs, a skylight should be located at opposite hips.

174 Attic conversions

10-19. Let the bathroom window do your decorating.

Emergency exits are required in attic living areas. The attic is a second story; your code might also require two exits, such as a second stairway. In any event, windows of sufficient size to permit exit to the outside should be provided. Some skylights qualify as egress windows, making it possible to convert hip-roof attics without having to add a dormer for window space or adding an outside entrance. Locate the lower end of the skylight no higher than 44 inches above the floor. Figure 10-21 shows the finished conversion of the attic shown in FIG. 10-14.

10-20. Bathroom storage is the key to order and efficiency.

Skylights

Skylights can be worked into almost any design to great advantage, providing ventilation, natural light and soft lighting. Skylights save on electricity, resulting in lower utility costs. Install low-E (low-emissivity) skylights. Low-E units comprise high-performance glass with a thin metallic coating that reflects radiant heat back to its source. This means that heat is reflected out of the house during warm days and into the house during cold days. Low-E glass, when compared with uncoated glass, is

10-21. Figure 10-14 becomes a comfortable place in which to retreat.

rated 72 percent better than single-glazing in reducing heat loss. It is 36 percent better than double-glazing and 14 percent better than triple-glazing. In direct sunlight, cooling efficiencies are rated 28 percent better than single-glazed uncoated glass and 19 percent better than double-glazed. It also reduces fading of drapes, furniture and carpeting caused by direct sunlight. As a general rule, the higher in the roof the skylight is positioned, the greater the spread of light. Figure 10-23 demonstrates how. Step-by-step skylight installation instructions are covered in Chapter 13.

THREE BASIC ATTIC CONVERSION PLANS

Figure 10-24 shows a basic attic conversion design for bedrooms and bathrooms with standard staircase. Figure 10-25 is a plan for a recreation room and half bath. A large attic can be converted into a two-bedroom apartment (see FIG. 10-26).

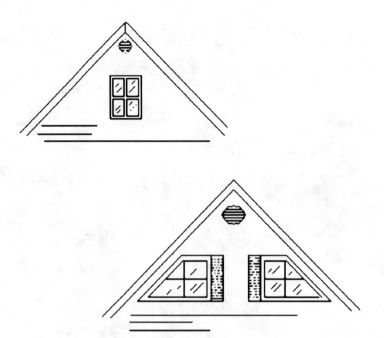

10-22. Install windows in the gable ends. You must have light and ventilation.

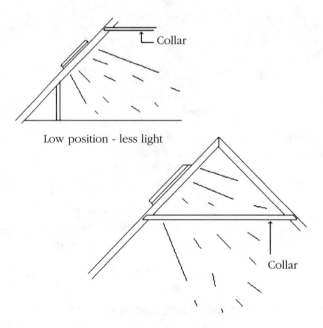

Collar

Low position - less light

High position - more light

10-23. Locate the skylight to suit your taste.

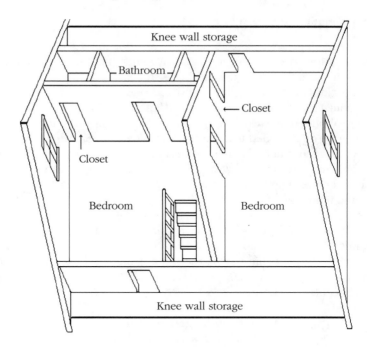

10-24. Making use of all available space.

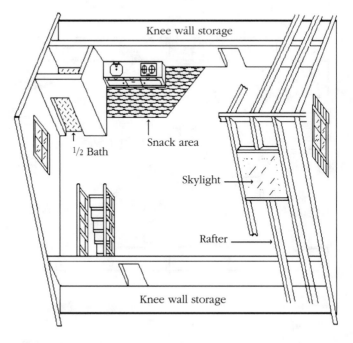

10-25. Turning unused attic space into a fun area.

ESTIMATING MATERIALS

When deciding how many reinforcement floor joists are required, count existing joists to determine quantity. Another method is to multiply the length of the attic by .75 and add one, for spacing 16 inches o.c. For 24 inch spacing, multiply attic by .5 and add one.

Estimate joist blocking by attic's length: a 36-inch attic length will require about 36 linear feet of blocking material for one run, 72 linear feet for the two runs needed to complete one side of the attic.

Subfloor and underlayment panels are computed by square feet. A 22 × 36 attic has 792 square feet and will require 25 4 × 8 feet panels. Do not deduct for the stairway because there will always be some waste in cutting and fitting panels.

A conventionally constructed knee wall (5 feet) requires a 10-foot 2 × 4 for two studs. A 36-foot wall requires 27 studs spaced 16 inches o.c. (fourteen, 10-foot 2 × 4s). You will need 2×4 sole and top plates for each knee wall. Again, using the 36-foot attic example, 72 linear feet of plate material is required, which equates to four, 2 × 4s 16 feet long and one 2 × 4 8 feet long.

See FIG. 10-10 to determine the best way to establish material requirements for nailers. The nailing ledger secured to rafter sides can be strips (1½ × 1¾ inch ripped from a 2 × 4. Materials for collars will depend on your ceiling design.

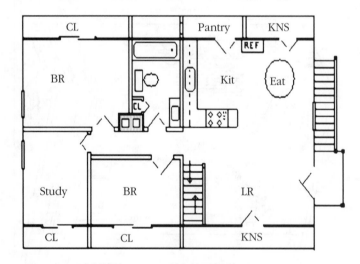

KNS - Knee wall storage
CL   - Closet

10-26. Income-producing conversion is possible.

A rule of thumb for estimating the number of studs required for a partition wall without openings is to multiply the length of the wall in feet by ¾ and add one piece. This gives the number of studs spaced 16 inches o.c.

For walls with a door opening and studs spaced 16 inches o.c., estimate one stud for each linear foot of wall. This allows for framing the opening. The bottom and top plates are computed the same as for a knee wall.

ESTIMATING YOUR LABOR HOURS

Estimating labor hours is guessing how much time it will take a reasonably skilled and experienced craftsperson to do a specific task. There are no two people with the same skill, experience and energy flow, so we base our guess on an average person.

More to the point: it will take you a good while to convert your attic. Allow a week to remove existing flooring, assuming the attic is the 22 × 36 dimensions used above. Remember, you are doing salvage work and not demolition; you want to save every board (or panel) and remove all nails. Be sure there is plenty of air circulating in the attic—do not attempt to work in a hot attic.

Joist reinforcement with 2 × 8s will take about 24 labor hours per 250 board feet. A 12-foot 2 × 8 has 16 board feet. Time includes moving material to the attic, sawing, fitting, and blocking. Allow the same time when installing 2 × 6s.

Replacing subflooring will take 17 labor hours per 500 board feet. Subfloor 4 × 8-inch panels will take 15 hours per 500 square feet. Partition and knee wall studding (including plates) can be estimated at 25 hours per 500 board feet. A 2 × 4 8-foot long has 5½ board feet. Compute adding collar beams at 25 hours per 200 board feet. Collar boxing with three pieces will take about 8 hours per 50 linear feet.

Chapter **11**

Windows
and doors

There are many types of doors and windows. Window technology has advanced to include insulating glass, glazing techniques that greatly reduce heat transmission; double-glazed windows with adjustable blinds enclosed between the panes that enable one to control the admission of light and shade; and a double-hung window that permits both sashes to tilt into the room for easy cleaning.

Exterior doors may be of insulated steel as well as traditional wood. In addition to embossed and raised panel designs, doors with hand carvings are available. Doors with stain and custom glass patterns are available at leading building supply houses. You might choose a paneled or louvered bifold door for interior openings; flush doors are also popular; and mirrored doors, glass sliding doors, and accordion doors are more options. French doors can be used to create a double-wide entrance and a captivating view (see FIG. 11-1).

Windows and skylights can be combined to give a room a feeling of openess and space, as shown in FIG. 11-2. Sometimes the best place to relax is in a quiet corner. Corner windows can give a wrap-around feeling from enveloping the observer in the view (see FIG. 11-3).

WINDOW TERMS AND CONSTRUCTION

The frame and sash are the basic components of any window. The frame encloses and supports the sash. The frame includes the side jambs (one on each side), the head jamb at the top, and the sill at the bottom of the frame.

The sash holds the glass in the frame. The vertical stiles on each side of the glass and the rails at top and bottom are parts of a sash. The bottom rail is wider than the other sash parts. Sashes can be single light or multilight. In multilight sashes bars (vertical or horizontal pieces running the full length of the sash) or mutins (short bars) divide the pieces of glass. To give a single-light sash the appearance of a multilight sash, use a

11-1. French doors work well in combinations of two.

11-2. Walls and ceilings do not have to be enclosures.

11-3. Think of a corner window as giving a room character.

snap-out grille. In a double-glazed light, the grille may be positioned between the glass.

The most common types of windows are:

- Double-hung
- Stationary
- Casement
- Horizontal sliding
- Awning

Frame and sashes can be made of wood or metal. Windows can be combined in different ways. A picture window is a large, stationary unit; you can surround it with other kinds of windows. A bow window is a series of windows in the shape of an arc. A bay window has its windows arranged in the shape of a polygon. A stacked window consists of several awning, hopper, or casement windows combined to make up a large glass area; opening units may be combined with stationary windows.

Insulated glass is used in both stationary and moveable sashes. It is formed with two or more sheets of glass, spaced apart and sealed air-tight.

Window terms and construction 185

Pella/Rolscreen Co.

Fine-grained Ponderosa pine, cedar, cypress, spruce and redwood are species used for window construction. The wood should be pressure treated with pesticide and water-repellent solution to ensure a long life.

Double-hung windows

The double-hung window has an upper and lower sash, both of which slide vertically in separate grooves in the side jambs, or in full-width metal weatherstripping. Each sash is held in any position with springs, balances, or compression weatherstripping. Figure 11-4 shows construction details of a double-hung window.

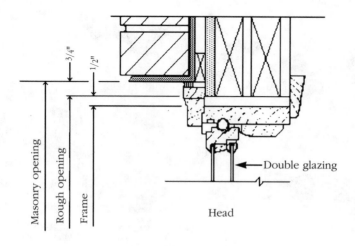

Head

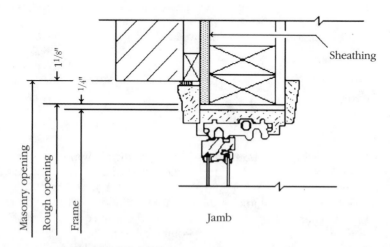

Jamb

11-4. Installation details showing a double-hung window in brick veneer construction.

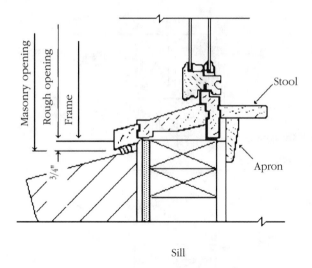

11-4. Continued.

Wooden double-hung windows have jambs (sides and top of the frames) made from nominal 1 inches lumber. The jambs are wide enough to use with drywall or a plastered interior finish. Sills are made from nominal 2 inch lumber. For good drainage, sills have about a 3-in-12 slope. Sashes are normally 1⅜-inches thick. Wooden windows are available with aluminum or vinyl exterior cladding.

Double-hung window sashes can be divided into a number of lights. For a Cape Cod or colonial-style house, sashes should be divided into six or eight lights. A ranch house looks best with top and bottom sashes divided into two horizontal lights. Some double-hungs are made with a single light in each sash and provided with a grille to divide it into lights. Snap-on grilles can be removed, which makes window washing easier.

To minimize air leakage, put building paper (15 lb. roofing felt) around the edges of the rough opening. Put the window into the opening. Plumb the frame with a level. Nail the window to the side studs and header through the casings (see FIG. 11-4) with corrosion-resistant nails.

A finger groove in the bottom rail eliminates the need for sash lifts. Install sash locks or fasteners in the center of the meeting rail. The sash lock draws the sash together when in lock position, giving a good air seal as well as securing the window closed.

Double-hung windows may be used as a single unit, doubled (mullion), or in groups of three or more. Double-hung windows may be used in a 30-degree, 45-degree, or 60-degree bay configuration.

Casement windows

Operating casement windows have side-hinged sashes that usually swing out. Figure 11-5 shows construction details. Casement windows are used as a single unit, as a pair, or in a combination of two or more. Casements are

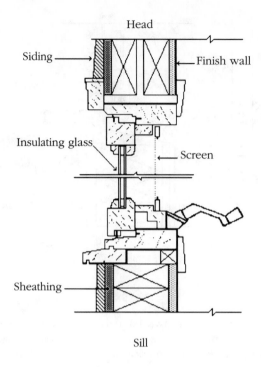

Head

Siding

Finish wall

Insulating glass

Screen

Sheathing

Sill

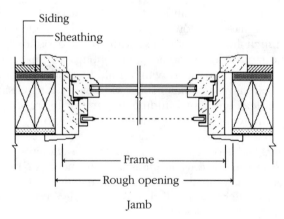

Siding

Sheathing

Frame

Rough opening

Jamb

11-5. Installation details showing casement window in siding wall.

also used to form casement radial bows and casement angular bays. Casements are available with double and single flankers (see FIG. 11-6).

Casement windows are available with insulating glass, low-E, tinted glass, and other options available in double-hung units. The whole window area can be opened for ventilation, whereas a double-hung unit provides only 50 percent open area.

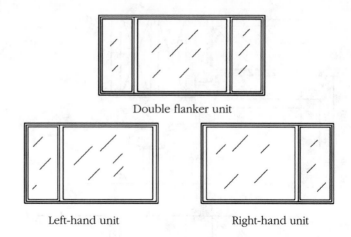

Double flanker unit

Left-hand unit   Right-hand unit

(As viewed from outside)

11-6. Casement windows with flankers.

Units are shipped from the factory completely assembled. The closing hardware consists of a rotary operator and sash lock. A snap-in grille or between-the-glass grille gives a multi-pane style for traditional homes. Casements are also available in stationary units.

Stationary windows

Stationary windows come in all styles and can be custom-built for almost any opening size and shape. They can be used alone, or in combination with double-hung, casement, round tops, and so on. Windows in 6–8-foot widths commonly use 1¾-inch-thick sashes for strength and to accommodate the thickness of insulating glass.

You can make a stationary window without a sash. Set the glass directly into rabbeted frame members, using stops to hold the glass in place. Putty the back and face of the glass to prevent moisture penetration.

Awning windows

The basic awning window consists of a frame in which one or more opening sashes are installed (see FIG. 11-7). Awning windows are available in wood, wood-clad, and metal. Awnings can be stacked vertically or combined side-by-side to create a wall of windows. Window combinations can be all fixed (non-vent) units, all vent units, or a combination of fixed and vent units. Awning units can, of course, be combined with other window types. Awning windows swing out at the bottom. A hopper window's top sash swings in at the top. Both awning and hopper units provide protection from rain when open.

Jambs are commonly 1¹⁄₁₆ inches or more thick because they are rabbeted. Sills should be at least 1⁵⁄₁₆ inches thick when two or more sashes are used in a complete frame. Each sash may, however, have its own individual

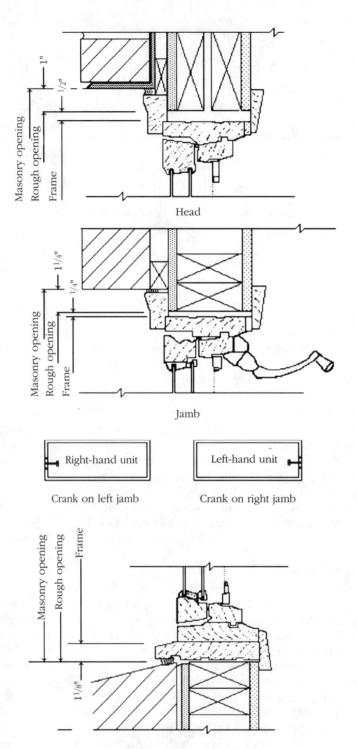

11-7. Installation details showing awning window in brick veneer wall.

frame, such as when it is used in combination widths and heights. Awning window units come with the same glass options available in other windows.

Horizontal-sliding windows

Horizontal-sliding windows resemble casement windows. The different is that the sashes, in pairs, slide by each other in tracks in the sill and head jamb. By using two or more units together, you can have multiple window openings. The windows are available in wood and in wood with aluminum cladding. Figure 11-8 contains construction details.

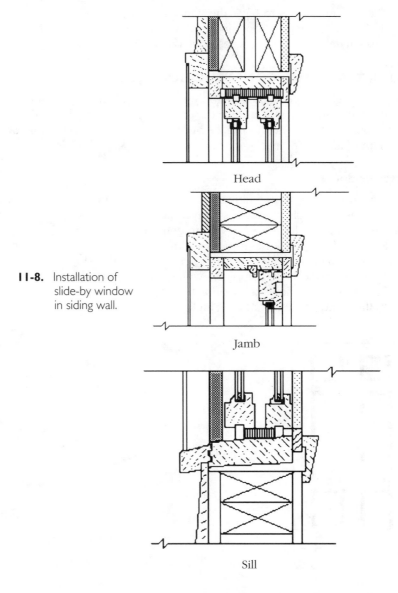

Head

Jamb

Sill

11-8. Installation of slide-by window in siding wall.

Determining window opening sizes

Rough opening sizes New windows are complete units when purchased at your local building supply store. A window comes complete with sash, frame and exterior trim. You usually pay extra for screens. As a general rule, find rough-opening sizes for windows as follows:

Double-hung windows, single unit The opening width equals the glass width plus 6 inches. The opening height equals glass height plus 10 inches.

Casement windows (two sashes) The opening width equals glass width plus 11¼ inches. The opening height equals glass height plus 6⅜ inches.

The safe practice is to have the window on hand (or physically measure it) before framing the opening. Not all manufacturers make their windows exactly alike and frame sizes do vary.

DOOR TERMS AND CONSTRUCTION

A tour through a large building supply house reveals many different door and entry designs. There is a door to suit almost every architectural whim. Once you choose a style, and make your purchase, be sure to store your doors upright, on end, in a dry area.

Exterior doors

Both exterior doors and combination (storm) doors are available in various designs to match the style of any house. A door with glass or side lights is appropriate for a house with an entry hall.

Exterior doors might have panels with solid vertical members (stiles), solid cross members (rails), and filler panels in various designs. Glazed (lights) upper panels are combined with raised wood or plywood lower panels. Figure 11-9 shows a traditional panel door. These doors are 1¾ inches thick and not less than 6' 8" high.

11-9. Traditional panel door.

A well-constructed door may be laminated with the wood core built up to 1⅛-inch thick with cross-banded wood layers and double aluminum vapor barriers permanently bonded to the wood with special adhesives, and hardwood outer layers, making the door very warp-resistant (see FIG. 11-10). Such a door may have interior and exterior oak veneer facing, and be prefinished sealed with a preservative and put through a multistep finishing process.

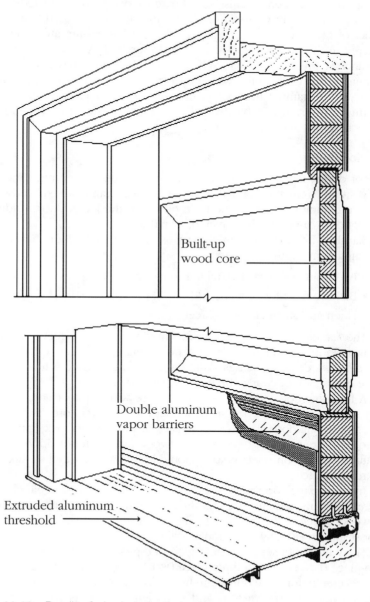

Built-up wood core

Double aluminum vapor barriers

Extruded aluminum threshold

11-10. Details of a laminated exterior door.

Prehung units come equipped with weather stripping. The exterior casing is fastened to a frame made of 1⅛-inch-thick or thicker wood. Rabbeting on the head and side jambs form stops for the door (FIGS. 11-10 and 11-11). The outside casing is wide enough to accommodate a 1⅛-inch combination or screen door.

Flush exterior wood doors commonly have a thin plywood face over a framework of wood, with a wood block or particleboard core. High-pressure laminate, hardboard, or composition face panels can be used in lieu of plywood. There are also metal exterior doors and insulated doors.

To install pre-hung exterior doors, nail the frame to the studs and header of the rough opening through the outside casing, after the unit is centered in the opening and leveled and plumbed. As a general rule, the sill can rest on the subfloor with a ⅝-inch-thick underlayment or wood flooring butted to the sill. Use a noncorrosive finish nail long enough to penetrate the framing member, a minimum of 1½ inches. After installing the finish floor, use a hardwood or metal threshold to fill the joint between the sill and finish floor.

Interior Doors

Interior doors, like exterior doors, come in a wide price range. There are many styles, from the plain flush door to fine, hand-carved hardwoods. The two common types are the flush door and the panel door. Folding or sliding doors can be flush, louvered, or paneled.

Standard interior doors are 1⅜ inches thick. Interior doors have a standard minimum width. They are:

- Bedroom and other habitable rooms—2 feet 6 inches
- Bathroom—2 feet 4 inches
- Linen and small closets—2 feet

The standard minimum height for interior doors is 6 feet 8 inches for the first floor; second floor interior doors may be 6 feet 6 inches high. Doors for wardrobes, such as sliding and folding, can be 6 feet or wider. These doors can, of course, be used in pairs or groups.

A flush interior door can be hollow core with a paper core, or it can be a solid core with a wood, particleboard, or mineral core. The face can be tempered hardboard, plastic laminate, or plywood of oak, gum, birch, mahogany, or any other type. Most plywood-faced interior doors can take a natural finish. Non-select grades should be painted, as well as those with a hardboard face.

Interior panel doors have the same parts as exterior panel doors. There are many designs available in a full range of sizes and in virtually all wood species. Bi-fold panels are also available. The colonial panel door shown in FIG. 11-9 is a popular style.

Many older houses were built with one-piece door frames (FIG. 11-12). Two-piece (FIG. 11-13) and three-piece (FIG. 11-14) versions came into being as a necessitity for developing pre-hung door units that are almost always installed in new construction and remodeling projects. Few carpenters hang doors to frames these days except when replacing a door.

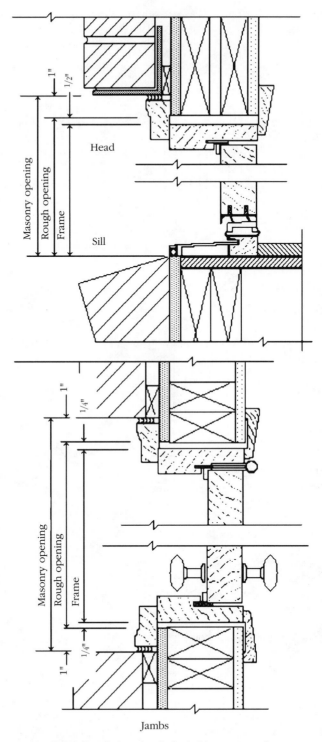

Masonry opening
Rough opening
Frame

1"
1/2"

Head

Sill

Masonry opening
Rough opening
Frame

1"
1/4"

1/4"
1"

Jambs

11-11. Door installation details for brick veneer wall.

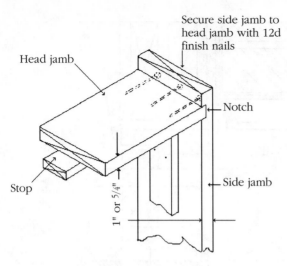

Secure side jamb to
head jamb with 12d
finish nails

Head jamb

Notch

Stop

1" or 5/4"

Side jamb

11-12. One-piece jamb.

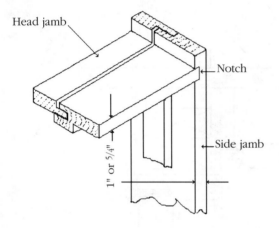

Head jamb

Notch

1" or 5/4"

Side jamb

11-13. Two-piece jamb.

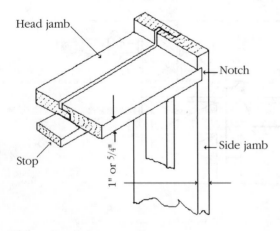

Head jamb

Notch

Stop

1" or 5/4"

Side jamb

11-14. Three-piece jamb.

The two-piece and three-piece adjustable jambs are adaptable to a variety of wall thicknesses. Pre-hung doors usually come with the casings installed with glue and staples.

Make the rough opening for interior doors 3 inches longer than the door height, and 2½ inches wider than the door width, which gives you the space needed to plumb and level the frame.

If you have standard openings, use a pre-hung door unless you'd prefer to build the frame and do the hanging yourself. Pre-hung single and double doors go directly into the opening. The pre-hung door is installed as a complete unit. Do not remove the door from the hinges. Before framing a door opening for a pre-hung unit, check with your building supply store to determine the exact rough opening size. Standard pre-hung door units are 6 feet 8 inches in height. You are safe when you frame the rough openings for interior doors 3 inches more than the door height and 2½ inches more than the door width. A common width for a closet door is 2 feet.

Interior doors should swing open in the direction of entry and, if possible, against an empty wall.

To install the pre-hung door unit:

1. Remove the packing nails connecting the keeper jamb, and separate the halves of the door frame (see FIG. 11-15).

2. Place the front half of the frame into the opening, as shown in FIG. 11-16. (The front half of the frame has the hinged door attached to

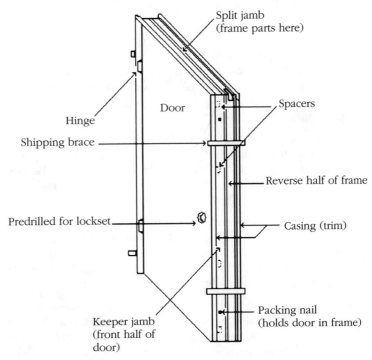

11-15. Ready to install pre-hung door unit.

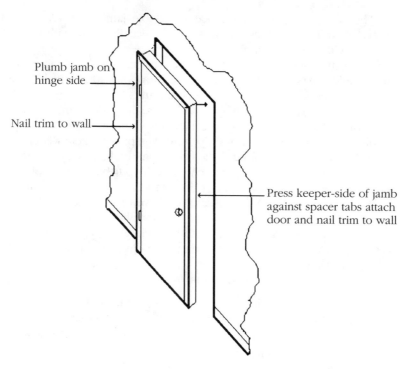

Plumb jamb on hinge side

Nail trim to wall

Press keeper-side of jamb against spacer tabs attach door and nail trim to wall

11-16. Installing front half of pre-hung door.

it.) Plumb the jamb on the hinge side of the frame. Using 6d casing nails spaced about 24 inches apart, nail the hinged-side trim to the wall. It is possible you might have to reposition the door, so do not drive the nails all the way in. At this point, you just want to "tack" the door in place.

3. Press the keeper side of the jamb firmly against the spacer tabs attached to the door edge. Check the head jamb for proper fit. The space between the top of the door and the jamb must be uniform. Nail the keeper-side trim to the wall with 6d casing nails spaced 24 inches. Do not drive in the nails all the way.

4. With the door closed and spaces still attached, shim behind the jamb. If the door unit is centered in the opening, thick shims should not be required. Use at least 3 shims to each side. Later, when door installation is complete, nail through the jambs and shims with 8d casing nails to firmly secure the unit.

5. Remove spacers and slide the reverse half of the frame into position, as illustrated in FIG. 11-17. Insert the top first. Next, press the sides firmly into position against the wall. Using 6d casing nails spaced 24 inches apart, nail through the trim into the wall. Do not drive nails all the way in.

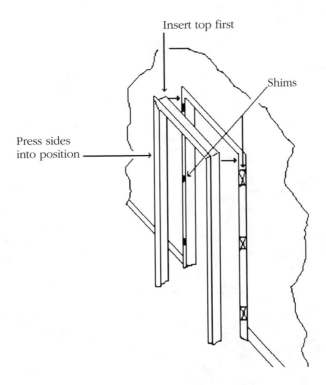

Insert top first

Shims

Press sides
into position

11-17. Installing reverse half of pre-hung door.

6. Recheck the plumb on the hinge side of the frame. Check the level of the head jamb. If these are satisfactory, install the lockset and keeper. The door should operate properly. If it doesn't locate the problem and correct it.

7. Drive and set all casing nails. Nail in place the side stops and header stops, using 3d finish nails spaced 12 inches apart.

Casing is the finish trim used around door and window openings to cover the juncture between the wall and jambs. Standard casing can be anywhere from 2¼ inches to 3½ inches wide depending on the style. It can be from half an inch to 1¼ inch thick or greater. The 1⅟₁₆-inch thickness is standard in many narrow patterns. Figure 11-18 shows two common patterns.

In attic conversions, knee walls and possibly other interior doors might not be standard height, and pre-hung units will not be available for these odd-size openings. You will have to build the frames and mount the door to the frame.

Nail the casings to both the jamb and the framing member (stud or header). Leave about a ³⁄₁₆-inch edge distance from the face of the jamb, as seen in FIG. 11-19. Set the nails in pairs and space the nails about 16 inches

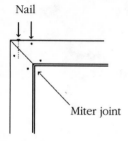

Nail

Miter joint

11-18. Two ways to fit casings.

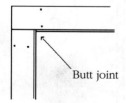

Butt joint

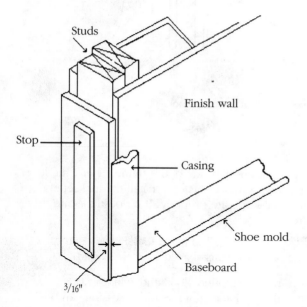

Studs

Finish wall

Stop

Casing

Shoe mold

Baseboard

3/16"

11-19. Door framing details.

apart along the full height of the opening and along the head jamb. Use finish or casing nails in 6d or 7d sizes, depending on the thickness of the casing. Use 4d finish nails (or ½-inch brads) to fasten the thinner edge of the casing to the jamb. Predrill hardwood casing for nails to prevent splitting.

Miter the corner joints of casing having a molded edge. Square-edge casing can be butt fitted at the corners but mitered corners are preferred (see FIG. 11-18).

Fitting door hardware

Figure 11-20 shows where to install the strike plate and where to place the door stops. Figure 11-21 shows how to install door hardware. Figure 11-22 gives you the normal clearances for exterior and interior doors. Leave a half-inch or larger gap under interior doors to allow sufficient air circulation in homes with central systems.

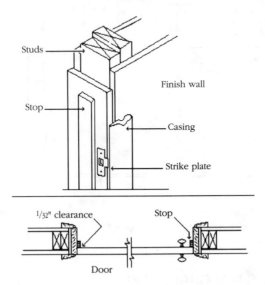

11-20. Strike plate installation and location of door stops.

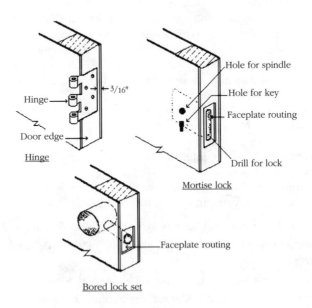

11-21. How to install door hardware.

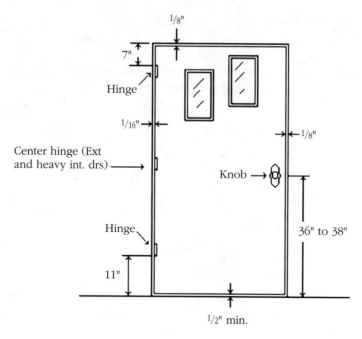

11-22. Installation specifications for doors.

DETERMINING MATERIALS AND ESTIMATING YOUR LABOR HOURS

Itemize your window and door requirements by type, size, and number needed. For doors, determine whether it is a *left-hand* door or *right-hand* door. (These terms indicate which way a door swings with respect to the hinged side when viewed from the outside. A right-hand door hinges on the right side when swinging away from you. A left-hand door has hinges on the left side and swings away from you.) List all hardware such as sash locks, screens, door locks, etc.

Order casing, stool, and apron material by the linear foot. A 6 feet 8 × 3 feet 0 inch door will require a 7-foot piece of casing for each side and about a 42-inch piece for the top. Avoid splicing casing.

Conventional window interior trim calls for casing at sides and top, stool, and apron at bottom.

The larger and heavier a window unit is, the longer it will take to install it. Here's what you can expect to accomplish:

- Double-hung unit and screen, size 3'4" wide × 5'2" high, 2 hours.
- Casement window and screen, size 3'10" wide × 4'2" high, two leaves, 1.5 hours.
- Picture window, size 4'6" wide × 4'6" high, 2.5 hours.
- Awning window, size 2'8" wide × 3'2" high, 1.5 hours.

These times include setting factory-made assembled windows in a prepared opening, plumbing and leveling with necessary shims, and securing with nails. Trim work is not included.

- Interior pre-hung door units, size 2'8" × 6'8", will take about 3 to 4 hours to install, including lockset.
- Bi-folding wood doors and vinyl covered wood doors, size 4'0" × 6'8", will take about 4 hours.
- Estimate exterior wood doors, size 3'0" × 6'8", at 4 hours, including hardware installation.

Interior trim work on doors and windows is, and should be, time-consuming, because you want to do it right. Allow two to three hours per window for casing, stool, and apron. Allow one hour to trim interior side of exterior doors.

Chapter **12**

Stairs

To reach that new attic "get-a-way", you must have a stairway. The stairs, as we saw in an earlier chapter, do not have to be against a wall but can be located almost anywhere. The stairs can be an attractive center point (see FIG. 12-1).

You can purchase most standard stairways precut and ready to assemble. Complete installation instructions and hardware is included. Many stair fabricators have catalogs that show the many different designs of the balusters, rails, and newels they have available. A well-designed stairway has graceful, well-proportioned, perfectly matched parts made of quality materials.

For the typical do-it-yourselfer, stair construction may appear to be too complicated. It isn't, as you will soon see. Let's start at the beginning.

Georgia-Pacific.

12-1. Make stairs a decorative part of the room.

COMING TO TERMS

It helps to understand the names of the various components of a thing before trying to build or fix that thing. Imagine how difficult it would be to become an automotive mechanic if you don't know what a carburator is or how it functions. Figure 12-2 illustrates some of the terms.

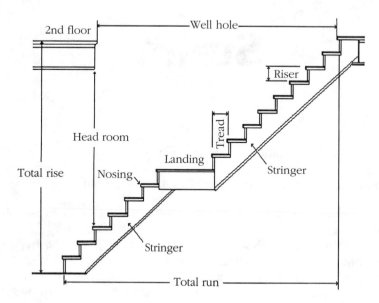

12-2. Basic stair terms.

A *staircase* is the whole set of stairs, including landings, winders, and stairs leading from one story to another. "Stairs" and "staircase" mean the same thing. A *flight of stairs* is a series of unbroken steps leading from one landing to another.

The *wellhole* is the framed opening in the floor of a building through which a stairway passes. The wellhole is guarded with balusters and a handrail if the stairway is open.

The *riser* is the upright member between two treads. The *tread* is the horizontal top surface where you step when going up or down the stairway. The tread may project a short distance in front of the riser to form a *nosing,* shown in FIG. 12-3. The tread of stairs has two parts: the run and the nosing. You do not consider the nosing when making stair calculations.

The *rise* of a step is the height from the top of one tread to the top of the next tread. The *run* of a step is the horizontal distance from the face of one riser to the face of the next riser. The run equals the width of a tread but not including the nosing.

The *total rise* of a flight of stairs is the height from finish floor to finish floor. It is the basic measurement for all stair layouts. It must be accurate,

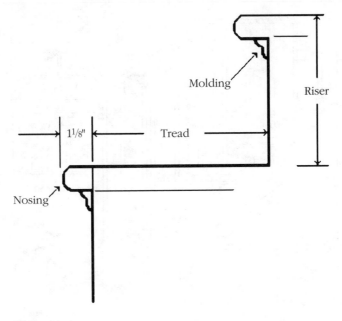

12-3. Nosing.

so you have to establish the measurement from the top of the finish flooring of both floors. It is unlikely that you will install the finish floor before building the stairs, so find out what the thickness of the finish floor will be and include that thickness in your calculations.

The *total run* of a flight of stairs is the horizontal distance from the face of the first riser to the face of the last riser in the same flight. It equals the sum of the treads. *Stringers* support the treads. The average small stairway, such as attic and basement stairs, has two stringers—one on each side of the treads. Three stringers are often used on main stairs leading from first floor to second floor. "Stringers," "string," "horses and carriages" can mean the same thing.

Headroom is the clearance above a stair. It is measured from the lowest point of the open end of the wellhole down to the outside corner of the tread and riser directly below.

The *handrail* is a plain or decorative piece that acts as a handrest and guide when descending or climbing the stairs. It is parallel to the stringer. The handrail is also used as a guard around the wellhole.

Balusters are the uprights installed between the rail and treads. They support the handrail and provide a side enclosure for the stairway. Balusters can be plain or decorated, square or round. A tread with 10–12 inches of run should have two evenly-spaced balusters (see FIG. 12-4).

A *newel post* is the finished post located at the bottom tread, at the top tread, and at the corners of the wellhole. Newels may be either solid or built-up, square or round, plain or fancy.

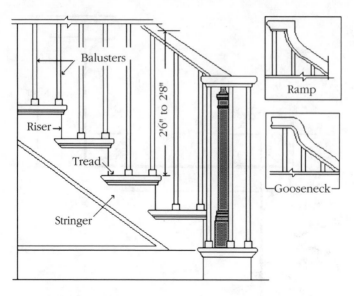

I2-4. Using two balusters to a tread.

A stairway may be designed with a continuous handrail and no in-between newel posts. Special curved pieces called *easements, goosenecks,* or *ramps* are used at the various turns of the stairway. The lower end of the railing may be finished with a wreath or spiral.

STAIRWAY LOCATION

Many stairways begin at a front hall in the center of the house. Such a stairway requires a large entrance hall. The average house does not have space for that much hallway, so the stairway is located in the living room. These stairs end in the hall on the second floor, never in a room.

It saves space if basement stairs are directly below the main stairs. Access to the basement stairs is generally from the kitchen area. Sometimes in two-story homes the attic stairs are directly over the main stairs. Such a design means the stairs and part of the attic space are visible from the hall below. Because of this visibility, the attic stairs should be made of quality materials. An alternative is to have a door at the foot of the attic stairs, which will take up some of the hall space on the second floor.

STAIRWAY TYPES

Straight and *platform* are the two most common types of stairways; see FIGS. 12-5 and 12-6. The straight-run stair is the simplest and least expensive to build because it leads from one floor to the next without turns or a landing.

Closed-string stairs are straight stairs with a wall on each side. Straight stairs with a wall on one side and a handrail or baluster on the other, as seen in FIG. 12-4, are called *open-string stairs.* You often see a straight-run

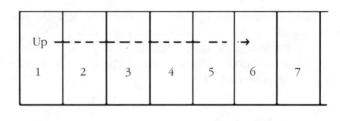

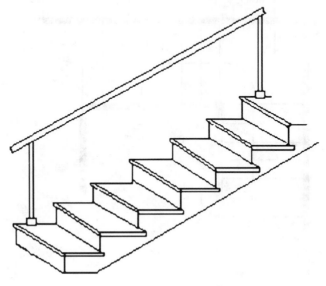

12-5. A straight stairway is simple construction.

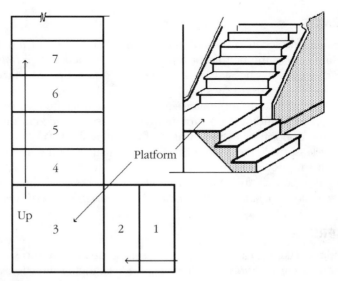

Platform

12-6. A platform stairway.

stairway open on both sides, with two balusters. Straight stairs need a long hallway and may not be possible in a small house.

The *platform stairway* has a change of direction part way up the stairs. It can start as an open-string stair and change to a closed-string stair after a few steps, as seen in FIG. 12-7.

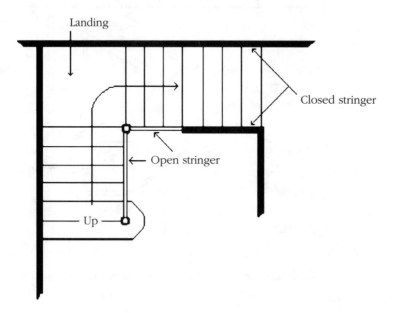

12-7. A stairway can have both open and closed stringers.

LANDINGS

The number and location of landings determine the name of the stairs. If the landing is near the bottom or top, the stair is called a *long L stair* or a *quarter-space stair*. The stair is L-shaped. In going up, you face a 90-degree turn. Figure 12-7 shows a long L with the landing near the bottom.

To fit a staircase into a limited space, build a U-shaped stairway. The stairs go up to a landing then turn 180 degrees, so the second flight continues in the opposite direction from the first flight, shown in FIG. 12-8. The landing, at least twice the width of the stairs, is usually at the middle of the staircase. It can, however, be closer to the top or to the bottom. A stairway of this kind, where the two flights have little space between them, is called a *narrow U stairs*, a *platform stair returning on itself*, or a *half-space stair*.

WINDERS

Stair landings take up valuable space, and some houses are too small for a stair with landings. *Winders* are steps used for changing directions. Figure 12-9 shows a common three-winder stairway. Many building codes prohib-

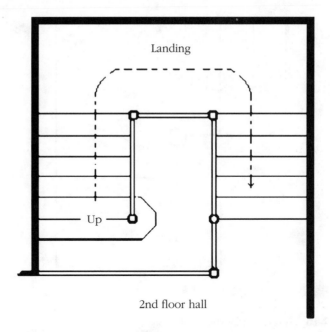

12-8. A U-shaped stairway.

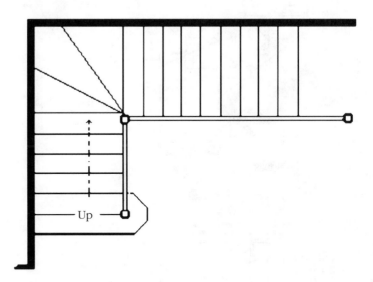

12-9. A typical winder stairway.

it this kind of stairway because the wide outside and narrow inside steps makes them somewhat dangerous; there is little or no tread for foot support at the inner corner, where all the winders meet. Also, the risers all come together at the inner corner, making a steep descent.

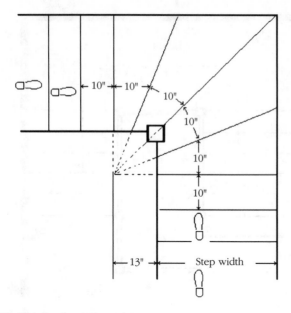

12-10. A safe winder stairway.

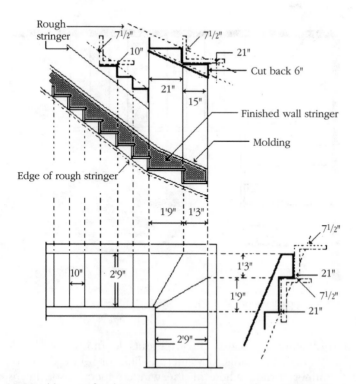

12-11. Use your framing square to lay out stringers for a winding stairway. The heavy lines indicate the shape of the stringer after cutting.

To overcome the problem use more winders, as shown in FIG. 12-10. Lay the steps out so they do not come to a point. Since most people walk about 14 to 16 inches from the inside when making the turn on stairs with winders, this arrangement has a tread width at the line of travel that's closer to the tread width of a normal step. The tread width at this point is 9 or 10 inches. Figure 12-11 shows how to lay out a stringer for a winding stair.

STAIRWAY WIDTH

The *width* of stairs is the distance between handrails, or between the wall and a handrail. A flight of stairs between floors should be at least 32 inches wide. Keep in mind that you will need to use the stairway to move furniture.

HEADROOM

The minimum *headroom* needed is 6'8". Look at FIG. 12-2 to see what headroom means. If there's more than one flight of stairs in the same stairwell, as in attic stairs over the main stairs, the design must allow enough headroom underneath the upper stair. Headroom is measured vertically from the top of a tread. Headroom will vary with the steepness of the stair, but is generally 7'4"–7'7". When contemplating your attic or basement conversion, determine the stairway design and construction details as one of the first items.

STRINGERS

A popular technique for constructing stairs is shown in FIG. 12-12. Often, finished boards are used to cover the carriage on the open-string stairs

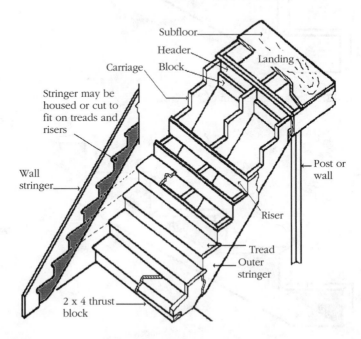

12-12. Stairway construction details.

and is usually called an *outer stringer.* (When a finished board is used on the wall side of the stairs, it's called a *wall stringer.*) When a finished board is grooved to receive the riser and tread (as in FIGS. 12-15 and 12-16), it's usually referred to as a *housed stringer.* There may be other names for carriage or stringer in your neighborhood, to further cloud the task of identifying stair components.

A *carriage* is usually made of 2-inch rough lumber (like a 2 × 12) cut so it makes a series of steps. The finished risers and treads are nailed to it. Wider stairs need three carriages. The two common kinds of stair carriages (or rough stringers) are: *sawed-out* and *built-up.* A sawed-out carriage is shown in FIG. 12-13. These are used for porch, basement, and attic stairs. The steps are sawn out of a piece of lumber that's wide enough to give support after it is cut, such as a 2 × 10 or 2 × 12. A built-up carriage is made by sawing triangular blocks from a 2-by and nailing them on 2 × 4 or 2 × 6 stock. The two triangle sides that are at right angles to each other are equal to the riser and tread of the stairway (see FIG. 12-14).

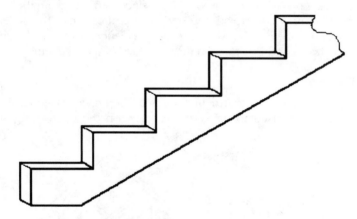

12-13. Carriage sawed out of 2-by stock.

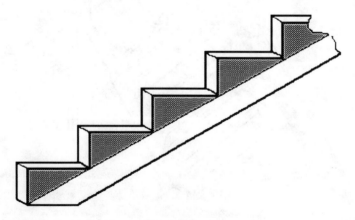

12-14. Carriage built up with triangular blocks.

Finished stringers are similar to a stair carriage but are made from finished stock. They are cut the same shape as a carriage, or cut on a miter for the riser cuts. Sometimes they're grooved, or *housed*. Housed stringers are used in quality stairs. The risers are rabbeted into the treads, then glued and nailed, as seen in FIGS. 12-15 and 12-16. The rabbeting and wedges make a stairway that is solid.

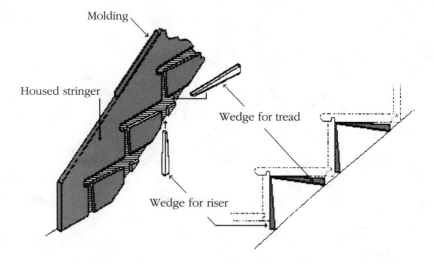

Molding

Housed stringer

Wedge for tread

Wedge for riser

12-15. Wedges glued into place make for firm construction.

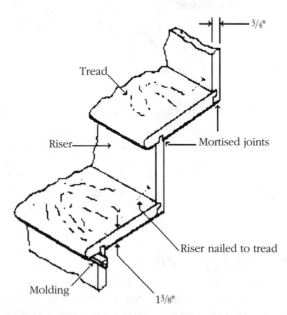

3/4"

Tread

Riser

Mortised joints

Riser nailed to tread

Molding

1³⁄₈"

12-16. Stairs with mortised joints and housed stringers are frequently used for main stairways.

ATTIC STAIRS

When stairs are open on one side, a railing and balusters are needed (see FIG. 12-17). Balusters are made with doweled ends that fit into drilled holes in the railing and in the treads. Balusters work best when fastened to tread ends and have finished returns. The railing can end at a newel post. An outer stringer and molding completes the stairway trim.

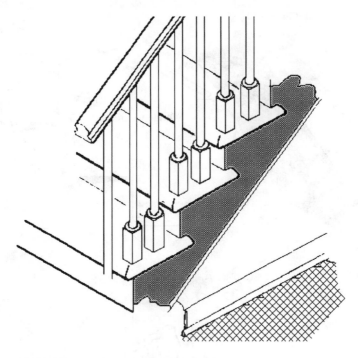

12-17. Open stairs to the converted attic.

A quality, fully-enclosed stairway is appropriate between the main floor and the attic. You can use a rough, notched carriage with a finished stringer, as illustrated in FIG. 12-18. Nail the stringer to the wall and then install the carriages. Cut treads and risers to fit snugly between the stringers, using finish nails to secure the treads and risers to the carriages. For an alternative method of installation, see FIG. 12-19. Begin by nailing the rough carriages directly to the wall and notch the stringers to fit the carriages. Install treads and risers as described above.

TREAD AND RISER DIMENSIONS

Closed interior stairs have a minimum tread width of 9 inches and a maximum riser height of 8¼ inches (FIG. 12-20). Exterior stairs, such as a flight of stairs up to your attic conversion, have a minimum tread of 11 inches and a maximum riser of 7½ inches.

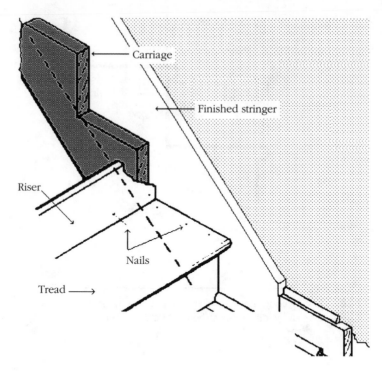

12-18. Using a notched carriage with a finished stringer.

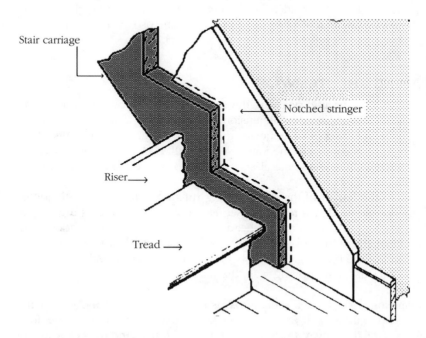

12-19. Using a notched stringer with a notched carriage.

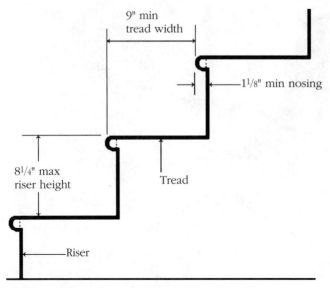

12-20. Building code requires minimum and maximum dimensions for tread width and riser height of closed stairs.

The ratio of riser to tread should permit a comfortable step. A 7½–8¼-inch riser will meet the requirement. A rule of thumb for the ratio between riser and tread is: The tread width in inches times the riser height in inches should equal 72 to 75. Another rule you can use is: The tread width plus twice the riser height should equal about 25.

FRAMING THE STAIRWAY

For a basement or attic stairway, the rough opening should be about 9'6" long by 32" wide. The long dimension of the opening can be either parallel to or at right angles to the joists. It is easier to frame an opening when the length runs parallel to the joists (see FIG. 12-21). A short header may be required for one or both ends. Use 16d nails to secure the header member to each joist.

When the length of the stair opening runs perpendicular to the joists, a long double-header is required (see FIG. 12-22). Joist hangers are a preferred method of anchoring the header and the joists to the header. You can add to the structural strength by building a load-bearing wall under part or all of the opening. The joists can then bear on the wall's top plate. If you don't use a supporting wall, the maximum allowable header length is 10 feet.

Framing for a long L stairway is usually supported in the basement. Use a load-bearing wall or use a post at the corner of the stair opening. When a similar stairway leads to the attic, frame the landing as shown in

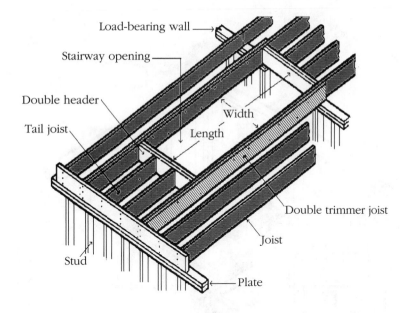

12-21. Framing parallel to rafters.

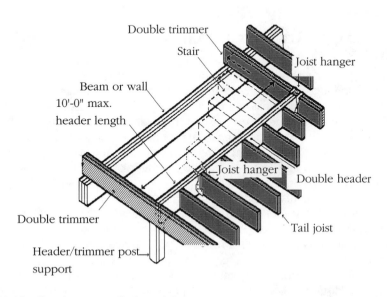

12-22. Framing perpendicular to joists.

FIG. 12-23. The landing frame is nailed to the wall studs and provides support for the stair carriages.

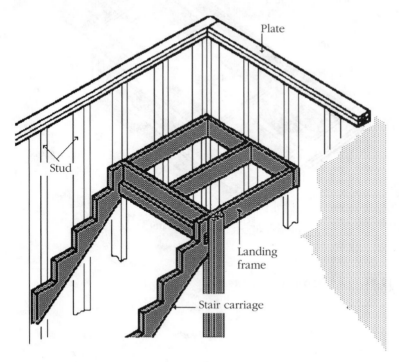

Plate

Stud

Landing frame

Stair carriage

12-23. Landing framing technique.

HOW TO LAY OUT A STAIR CARRIAGE

Figure 12-24 gives the dimensions for various heights of straight stairs. Figure 12-25 gives the dimensions for stairs with landings. As you can see, the key measurements are given. Assuming that you have already calculated the tread and riser dimensions, the next step is to establish the carriage dimensions. It takes time to establish carriage dimensions so when selecting lumber for the layout task, make certain the piece is long enough. Figure 12-26 shows the different between the mathematical carriage length and the actual carriage length. The actual length of the carriage can't be known until the layout is completed.

To find the mathematical carriage length with a steel square, do this: locate, on the body of the square, the total run (in feet) (refer to the dimensions given in FIG. 12-24). On the tongue of the square, locate the floor-to-floor height (in feet). Measure the distance between these two points on the square. This distance will be the approximate carriage length.

Let's do an example: the total run is 10'6" and the floor-to-floor height is 9'6". The distance between 10'6" on the body of the square and 9'6" on the tongue measures about 14'2", so we will use a 16-foot board for the

Height Floor-to-Floor-H	Number of Risers	Height of Risers R	Width of Risers T	Total Run L	Minimum Headroom Y	Well Opening U
	12	8"	9"	8'3"	6'6"	8'1"
8'-0"	13	$7^3/_8$"+	$9^1/_2$"	9'6"	6'6"	$9'2^1/_2$"
	13	$7^3/_8$"+	10"	10'0"	6'6"	$9'8^1/_2$"
	13	$7^7/_8$"-	9"	9'0"	6'6"	8'3"
8'-6"	14	$7^5/_{16}$"-	$9^1/_2$"	$10'3^1/_2$"	6'6"	9'4"
	14	$7^5/_{16}$"-	10"	10'10"	6'6"	9'10"
	14	$7^{11}/_{16}$"+	9"	9'9"	6'6"	8'5"
9'-0"	15	$7^3/_{16}$"+	$9^1/_2$"	11'1"	6'6"	9'6-12"
	15	$7^3/_{16}$"+	10"	11'8"	6'6"	$9'11^1/_2$"
	15	$7^5/_8$"-	9"	10'6"	6'6"	$8'6^1/_2$"
9'-6"	16	$7^1/_8$"	$9^1/_2$"	$11'10^1/_2$"	6'6"	9'7"
	16	$7^1/_8$"	10"	12'6"	6'6"	10'1"

"U" dimensions based on 6'6" min. headroom.
If headroom is increased well opening also increases.

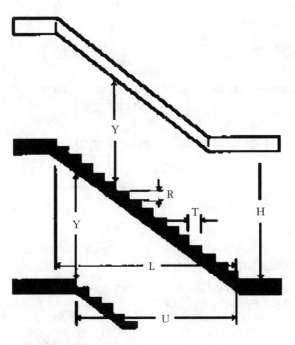

12-24. Dimensions for straight stairs.

Height Floor-to-Floor H	Number of Risers	Height of Risers R	Width of Tread T	Run Number of Risers	L	Run Number of Risers	L2
8'0"	13	7³/₈"+	10"	11	8'4"+W	2	0'10"+W
8'6"	14	7⁵/₁₆"-	10"	12	9'2"+W	2	0'10"+W
9'0"	15	7³/₁₆"+	10"	13	10'0"+W	2	0'10"+W
9'6"	16	7¹/₈"	10"	14	10'10"+W	2	0'10"+W

Stairs with landings take up less stair space and provide a resting point and a logical place for a right-angle turn.

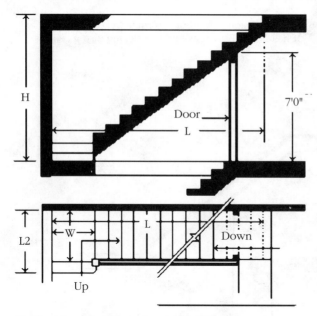

12-25. Dimensions for stairs with landings.

carriage. A 14-footer is not longer enough because the stock should be 18–20 inches longer than the carriage length.

1. Place the carriage board on a pair of saw horses. The right-angle portion of the square should be toward you, as seen in FIG. 12-27. On the body of the square, locate the number representing the tread width (9 inches in our example. Also see FIG. 12-24). On the tongue of the square locate the riser height, 7⅜ inches in our example.

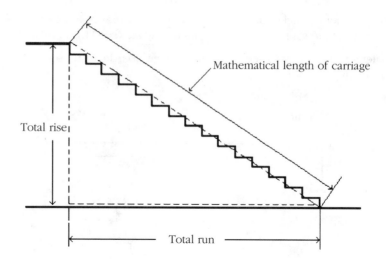

12-26. Finding the mathematical carriage length.

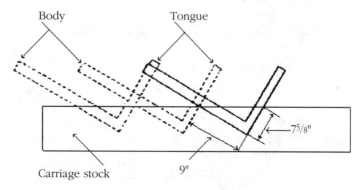

12-27. Beginning the carriage layout.

2. Beginning at the end of the board, place the square so these two numbers intersect the top edge of the board (FIG. 12-27). Mark a line along the outside edges of the square. Now move the square to the next step, shown in FIG. 12-27.

3. Continue laying out the steps until all treads and risers are marked. The number of treads is always one less than the risers. In our example there are 15 risers. Number each riser to make sure you have the correct number.

4. Cut the carriage board along the lines marked. Allow for the thickness of one tread when cutting the first step. If the treads are

1½ inches thick, cut 1½ inches from the bottom of the carriage so the entire stairway will be 1½ inches lower (see FIG. 12-28).

Refer to FIG. 12-29 to see how the carriage board can be secured to the floor framing.

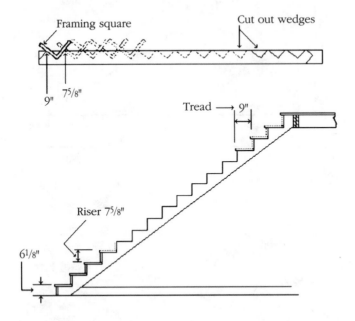

12-28. Steps for laying out a stairway.

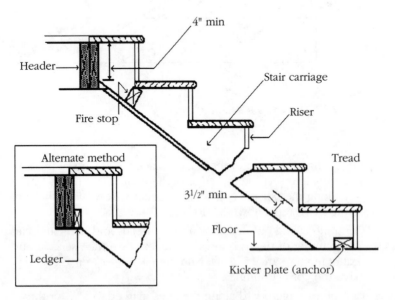

12-29. Securing stair carriage to floor.

DETERMINING MATERIALS AND ESTIMATING YOUR LABOR HOURS

Having determined the stair dimensions and type, you can estimate the materials. Use TABLE 12-1 as a guide to listing and pricing materials. These estimates are based on the assumption that the opening for the stairway is already framed and the subfloor in place.

Table 12-1   Stair materials.

1. Stairs required: Basement_____ Attic_____
2. Stair type: Straight_____ Long "L"_____ Narrow "U"_____
                Winders_____ Landing_____
3. Stair dimensions:
       Floor to floor_____ number of risers_____
       height of risers_____ width of treads_____
       total run_____ minimum headroom_____
4. Number of carriages (or stringers)
       Two_____ three_____
5. Number of handrails:
       One_____ two_____
6. Stairway is:
       Open_____
          railing_____
          balusters_____
          newel posts_____
       Closed_____
          handrail_____
7. Materials and costs:
       Carriages:
          2×10 _____ BF @ $_____ BF=$_____
          2×12 _____BF @ $_____ BF=$_____
       Stringers:
          $^{25}\!/_{32}$" _____BF @ $_____ BF=$_____
          $^{7}\!/_{16}$" _____BF @ $_____ BF=$_____
       Treads:
          $1^{11}\!/_{16}$" _____BF @ $_____ BF=$_____
          $1\frac{1}{2}$" _____BF @ $_____ BF=$_____
          $1\frac{5}{8}$" _____BF @ $_____ BF=$_____
       Risers:
          $^{25}\!/_{32}$" _____BF @ $_____ BF=$_____
          1" _____ BF @ $_____ BF=$_____
       Handrail _____LF @ $_____LF=$_____
       Newel posts _____Ea @ $_____Ea=$_____
       Balusters _____Ea @ $_____Ea=$_____
       Molding _____LF @ $_____LF=$_____
       Nails _____Lbs @ $_____lb=$_____
       Framing and bracing:
          2×8 _____BF @ $_____ BF=$_____
          2×6 _____BF @ $_____ BF=$_____

2 × 4 _____BF @ $_____BF=$_____
Prefabricated stairs: $_____
Other materials:

_____ _____ @ $_____ =$_____
_____ _____ @ $_____ =$_____
_____ _____ @ $_____ =$_____
Total costs $_____

An experienced carpenter can build a plain, straight stairway to your attic in 8–16 hours. It will take most do-it-yourselfers twice that time, or longer. The same carpenter can be expected to build two short flights in 10–12 hours. You might want to allow yourself 18–24 hours. Allow 16–24 hours to install newels, balusters and handrails for plain stairs. When installing prefabricated, straight wood stairs, allow yourself at least 8 hours.

Chapter 13

Skylights

What's available in skylights? Almost everything. There are units that rotate—topside down—to make cleaning the top from the inside easy; units with a ventilation flap so fresh air can enter even when the unit is closed; another style has an optional semi-transparent exterior awning easily attached to the window that remains hidden when not in use. You do not have to climb on the roof to install one model; the sash lifts out and you can install the unit from the inside—a terrific advantage if your roof slopes steeply.

Many skylights that open have integrated insect screens. Some have manual or motorized control rods for opening and closing windows installed beyond arm's length. You can spend a little more and get a skylight with an electric control system that lets you open and close the unit and operate venetian blinds with the touch of a button. For further convenience and protection, the unit has a sensor that automatically closes the unit when it begins to rain.

Shades, blinds and awnings are available for some models. Choices in glazing range from single dome to multidomes with tempered, low-E argon gas-filled, bronze-tinted glass to control heat transmission, light, and ultraviolet rays. Figure 13-1 shows how a skylight sprays a room with inviting rays of sunshine.

SELECTING THE RIGHT SKYLIGHT

Figure 13-2 shows two skylights installed in an attic bedroom. The two windows were installed instead of building a dormer. As a general rule, the glass area of the skylight should be a minimum, 10–15 percent of the room's floor space. You can make a small space appear larger and airier by installing a larger window to bring in more light.

The pitch of the roof should be considered as well as the height of the window. If you plan to install the skylight eye level on a low-sloping roof, select a taller window size. The roof's low slope reduces the field of

13-1. Use skylights to save energy and brighten a room.

Dal-Tile Corp.

vision. A taller unit can compensate for the loss (see FIG. 13-3). Skylights in the attic can be installed at the knee wall to permit eye-level view of the outside (see FIG. 13-4).

Skylights are available that fit between rafters spaced 16 and 24 inches on center. If you plan to install a wider skylight, some modification of the rafters will be necessary (see FIG. 13-5).

Cut the obstructing rafter for an opening, as shown in FIGS. 13-5 and 13-6. When more than one rafter is cut, double the headers to reinforce the roof. Use three 16d nails to secure the header member to each rafter.

Daily activities such as cooking, clothes and dish washing, showers, tub baths, etc., cause a build-up of moisture in the house, which in turn can create condensation on skylights. Ventilating units can help reduce condensation problems by passing fresh air in and stale air out. Keeping the interior glass panes warmer can also help. Install a heating source below the window and operate a ceiling fan to circulate the warm air (see FIG. 13-7). To further prevent condensation, surround the skylight and shaft with insulation with same R-value as in the ceiling.

THE SKYLIGHT SHAFT AND HOW TO FRAME IT

Attic skylights do not need a shaft if they are installed in a ceiling fixed directly to the rafters, as in FIGS. 13-2 and 13-4. When installing a skylight in a conventional ceiling, a shaft is necessary. Figure 13-8 shows two shaft designs. A beveled shaft might be required in order to remove the insect

13-2. Install skylights instead of building a dormer.

screen on some models. A straight shaft works best for a direct, overhead concentration of light. To distribute the light over a broader area, change the angle of the shaft (see FIG. 13-9).

Think of the shaft as a framed box. You want to accurately locate its position before removing the finish ceiling in the shaft area. Study FIG. 13-10 to determine your shaft location and construction details.

The skylight shaft and how to frame it 229

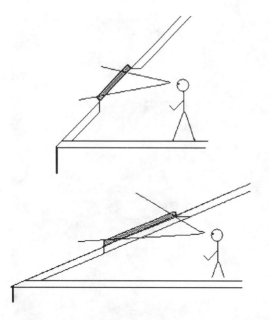

13-3. Low-sloping roofs require taller skylights for eye-level viewing.

Velux-American, Inc.

13-4. An eye-level view adds to the "openness" of an attic conversion.

Insulate the shaft with fiber glass batts. Staple the batts between the framing, keeping the vapor barrier facing the shaft (heated side). Finish the shaft with wallboard, plywood, hardboard or the same material as the ceiling. Paint the shaft white or a light color to reflect light.

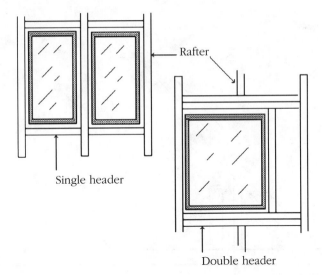

13-5. Install skylight between rafters or modify rafters for wider units.

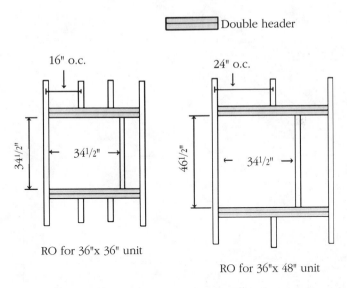

13-6. Reinforce openings in rafters with double headers.

HOW TO INSTALL A SKYLIGHT

For this job we will be installing a single type, curb-mounted skylight. Curb-mounted units have, as the name implies, a curb. Flush-mounted or self-flashing units are installed directly on a pitched roof, as we shall later discuss. For this particular unit, your roof slope must have a ³⁄₁₂ or greater pitch.

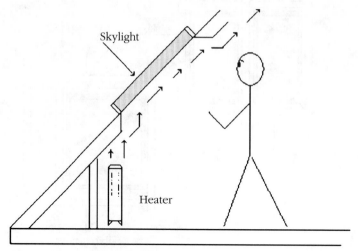

13-7. Circulate warm air to control condensation.

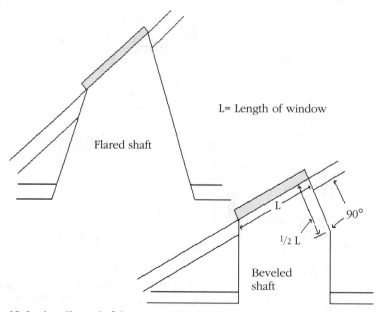

13-8. Installing a shaft in a conventional ceiling.

Most skylights come packaged with installation instructions and the parts necessary to install it. Not all skylights are made alike, and therefore may require slightly different steps for installation. For this job we will be using a common brand of skylight. Let's open the package and see what it contains:

- Installation instructions, which we will be using.
- Skylight with an attached rubber boot.

- Support brackets—four or more depending on skylight size.
- #8 × ⅞" Phillips screws (two per bracket).
- #8 × 2" screws (two per bracket).
- Roll(s) of waterproof tape.
- 4 counterflashings (fixed skylights supplied with 4 #6 × ¼" screws).

In addition, you will need:

- Lumber and wallboard for shaft construction.
- Replacement shingles, roofing felt, roofing cement, and nails.

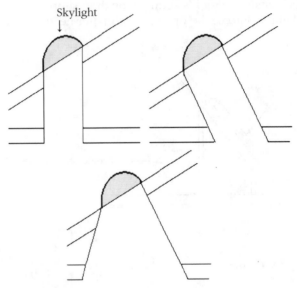

13-9. Use shaft to control light direction.

It always helps to know what tools are required to do a job. The installation instructions list the following tools needed to install the sky-light: Phillips screwdriver with #2 bit; tape measure; level; hammer; 12-inch-long block of wood (2 × 4); stiff blade putty knife; tinsnips or utility knife; power saw; hand saws (keyhole and crosscut); plumb bob; nail puller; two ladders.

Do not make a critical mistake and start cutting through the roof or ceiling without first making sure electrical wiring, plumbing pipes, and all other wires are removed. Always assume that there is a wire or pipe where you plan to cut—most of the time there will be.

1. Determine exactly where the skylight is going to be located in the ceiling. Now stop, sit down with a cup of coffee or a glass of iced tea, and think about what you are doing. Are you absolutely certain you have considered all the details, including the weather?

2. Mark the location of the four corners of the skylight on the underside of the roof by driving nails up through the roof. When installing more than one skylight of this type, you need at least 6 inches between the skylights to seal the rubber boots.

3. Go up onto the roof and snap a chalk line from nail to nail, marking the outline of the opening. The opening must be ½-inch larger than the skylight frame, giving a ¼-inch clearance on each side. Remove the shingles and then the nails in the path of your saw. Cut out the opening (do not let the cut pieces fall onto the ceiling). If one or more rafters are going to be cut, install structural bracing before cutting.

4. Make certain the roof is strong enough to support you and the skylight. Reinforce the opening with rafter headers (see FIG. 13-6).

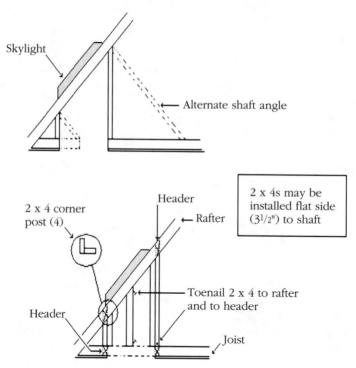

13-10. Skylight shaft framing technique.

Most skylights are heavy and the smart do-it-yourselfer gets help to carry the unit onto the roof and place it in position. Then follow these steps:

1. Install all the support brackets provided in the grooves on the two longest sides of the skylight, as shown in FIG. 13-11. Secure the brackets using two #8 × ⅞" screws (provided) per bracket.

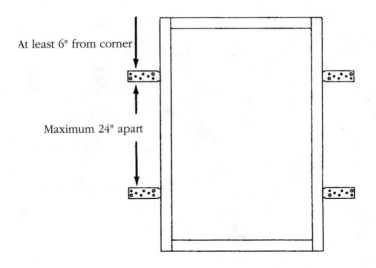

At least 6" from corner

Maximum 24" apart

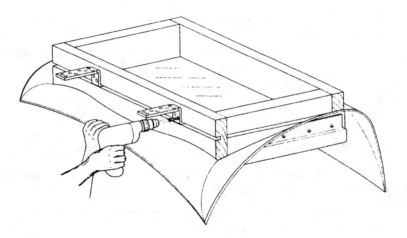

13-11. Installing support brackets. Pella/Rolscreen Co.

2. Place the skylight in the opening with the condensation gutter on the bottom (down the slope); see FIG. 13-12. Do not turn the unit sideways—flashings will not fit properly and may cause leaks.

3. Check that the skylight is square by measuring diagonally from opposite corners. The diagonal dimensions should be the same. A framing square may also be used to check for squareness.

4. Make sure unit is level (side to side) across the sill (bottom) and across the head (top). Vent units will not seal properly if the frame is not square and level. If the frame is not level, add solid blocking or shims between the support brackets and roof.

   A word of caution here: When installing skylights with tempered glass, metal tools and sharp objects (even small stones) may scratch

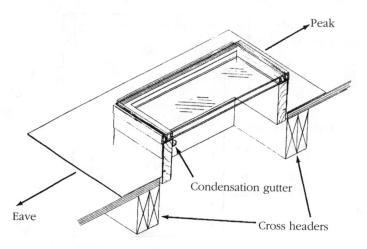

Peak

Condensation gutter

Eave

Cross headers

13-12. Placing the skylight in the proper position ensures trouble-free performance. Pella/Rolscreen Co.

the glass. Scratches in tempered glass may result in immediate or delayed breakage.

5. Secure the brackets to the roof using two #8 x 2-inch stainless steel screws (provided) in each bracket, as seen in FIG. 13-13. The screws must penetrate the rafters.

6. If a venting skylight is being installed, open it and remove the shipping spacers between the sash and frame. Now close the skylight. If it does not operate well, go back to step 3, above.

7. You are now ready to replace shingles and install the flashing.

The type of shingles on your roof will dictate how the unit will be installed. On roofs covered with asphalt or fiberglass shingles:

1. Make certain the rubber boot overlaps the roofing felt. If roofing felt covers the boot, leaks are likely.

2. Lay shingles up to the bottom of the skylight, and slide shingles under (not over) the rubber boot, as illustrated in FIG. 13-14.

3. Use the waterproof tape (provided) to seal the rubber boot to the shingles and roofing felt. Start across the bottom and then tape up the sides. Finally, tape across the top. Make sure to overlap at the corners. The waterproof tape may not stick well in cold weather. If you find this to be the case, nail or staple the tape to the roof to secure it.

4. Finish shingling the roof. Use roofing cement to seal shingles to the rubber boot to keep water from flowing sideways under the shingles. Be sure the shingles cover the waterproof tape and boot on all four sides of the skylight. You may nail through the rubber boot, but stay at least 3 inches from the edge of the skylight. Do not cut the rubber boot.

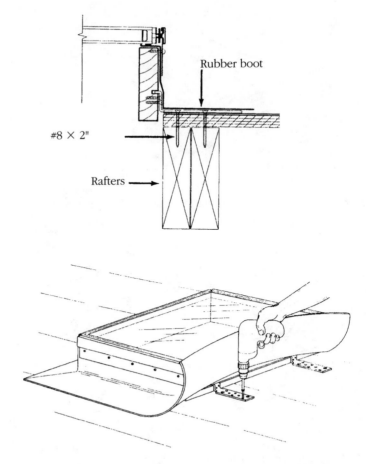

Rubber boot

#8 × 2"

Rafters

13-13. A skylight is not adequately secured unless anchor screws penetrate rafters. Pella/Rolscreen Co.

HOW TO INSTALL COUNTERFLASHING

The skylight package contains four lengths of counterflashing. The two pieces sized for the left and right sides of the unit are the same. The counterflashing with the attached water deflector is the head piece, and is installed at the top of the skylight.

When installing fixed units do this:

1. Remove the release paper from the foam tape on the sill counterflashing. Center it on the bottom of the skylight and drive it into the receiving groove on the face of the unit. Use a block of wood to protect the counterflashing. Striking the flashing with a hammer will cause unsightly dents (see FIG. 13-15).

2. Install the side (jamb) counterflashings as illustrated in FIG. 13-16. NOTE: If you used wood or slate shingles and did not allow enough room for the counterflashings to fit between the unit and the shingles, simply cut off up to 1 inch of the counterflashing.

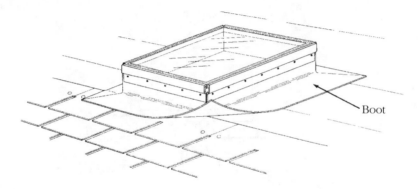

13-14. A skylight will leak if not properly installed. Pella/Rolscreen Co.

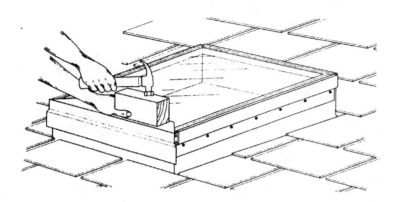

13-15. Use a wood block to tap counterflashing in place. Pella/Rolscreen Co.

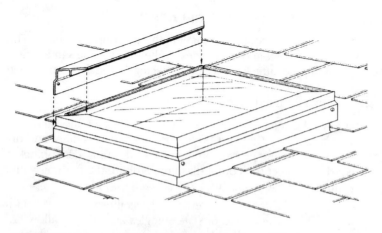

13-16. Side pieces go on next. Pella/Rolscreen Co.

3. The head counterflashing with water deflector is installed last (see FIG. 13-17).

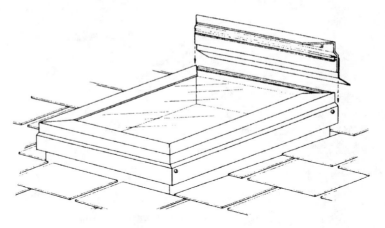

13-17. The head (top) piece follows. Pella/Rolscreen Co.

4. The ends of the counterflashings should meet at the corners. Secure the counterflashings with one #6 × 1¼" screw (provided) at each corner (see FIG. 13-18).

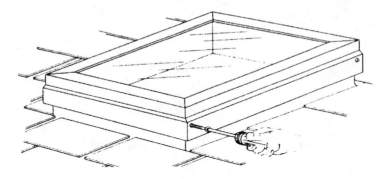

13-18. Do not overtighten counterflashing screws. Pella/Rolscreen Co.

5. Loosen the adjusting screws on the head counterflashing and adjust the water deflector down tight against the shingles and tighten the screws (see FIG. 13-19).

HOW TO INSTALL STEP FLASHING WITH WOOD SHINGLES

For wood shake or slate shingles you may have to make minor modifications to adjust for the additional thickness of the shingles. The flashing pieces used in this installation are shown in FIG. 13-20.

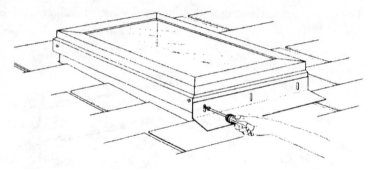

13-19. Be sure the water deflector fits snugly against the shingles.
Pella/Rolscreen Co.

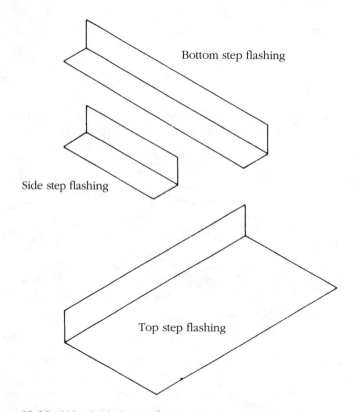

Bottom step flashing

Side step flashing

Top step flashing

13-20. Wood shingle step flashing pieces. Pella/Rolscreen Co.

It is important that the skylight be installed on solid sheathing covered with overlapping felt. The three types of step flashing needed to complete these instructions are contained in some package. Here's how to do it:

1. Tape the rubber boot to the roofing felt using the waterproof tape supplied with the skylight. This procedure is the same as for

asphalt shingles, except that the waterproof tape does not overlap the bottom row of shingles.

2. After applying waterproof tape, shingle up to the bottom of the skylight (see FIG. 13-21).

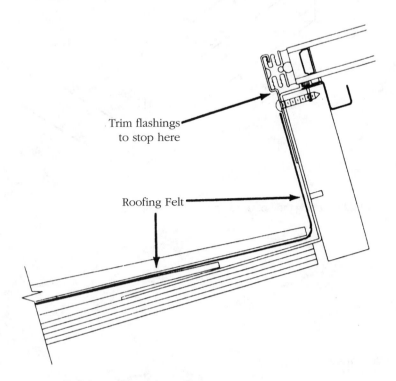

Trim flashings to stop here

Roofing Felt

13-21. Forming a tight seal. Pella/Rolscreen Co.

3. Cut the bottom step flashing to length—the width of the unit plus 10 inches. Cut the vertical leg 5 inches from each end and fold down the ends, as illustrated in FIG. 13-22.

4. Trim the vertical leg of the bottom flashing to fit the height of skylight. Be sure to note the difference of 1 inch between fixed and vent units. The flashing should cover the screws that secure the rubber boot, but should extend no higher than the lip above the screws (see FIG. 13-21).

5. Place the bottom flashing against the skylight, as shown in FIG. 13-23.

6. Trim, notch, and bend pieces of step flashing so the vertical legs wrap around the lower corners of the skylight on each side. Side flashings overlap the bottom flashing as seen in FIG. 13-23.

7. Before placing side flashings against the skylight, trim off the tops of the vertical legs so they are flush with the lip above the boot screws (see FIG. 13-21).

How to install step lashing with wood shingles 241

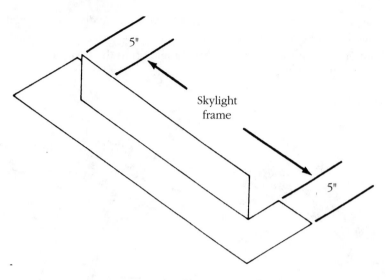

13-22. Cutting the bottom step flashing. Pella/Rolscreen Co.

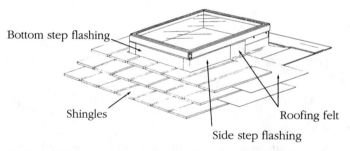

Bottom step flashing

Shingles

Roofing felt

Side step flashing

13-23. Follow each step carefully for a water-tight skylight.
Pella/Rolscreen Co.

8. When the side flashings are installed, lay the next course of roofing felt and shingles (see FIG. 13-24). Be sure to lap felt up the sides of the skylight frame. When installing the shingles, keep shingles back an inch from the sides of the unit (see FIG. 13-25).

9. Install additional pieces of side flashing, trimming the vertical legs to fit just above the boot screws as depicted in FIG. 13-21. Overlap the previously installed lengths of side flashing. Continue laying felt, shingles and flashing up to the top of the unit, as shown in FIG. 13-26).

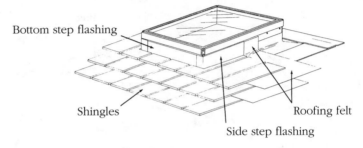

Bottom step flashing

Shingles

Roofing felt

Side step flashing

13-24. Proper installation of roofing felt is key to preventing leaks.
Pella/Rolscreen Co.

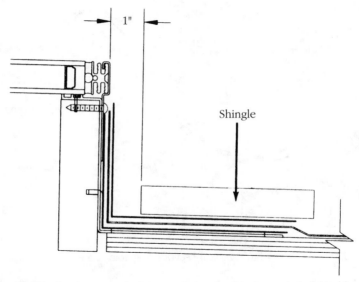

1"

Shingle

13-25. Leave a one inch space between shingles and skylight sides.
Pella/Rolscreen Co.

10. Trim, notch, and bend the last piece of side flashing on each side so the vertical legs fold around the upper corners of the skylight (see FIG. 13-27).

11. Cut the top step flashing to length—width of the skylight plus 10 inches. Trim, notch and bend the ends to fit over the side flashings (FIG. 13-27). Trim the vertical legs to fit just above the boot screws.

12. When the top flashing is in place, finish replacing the shingles.

13. Apply a bead of quality silicone sealant to the joint between the step flashings and skylight. Seal all the way around the unit.

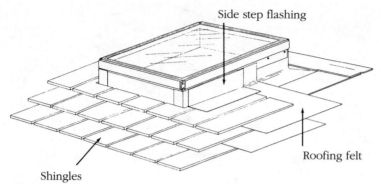

13-26. Keep laying flashing, roofing felt, and shingles toward the top.
Pella/Rolscreen Co.

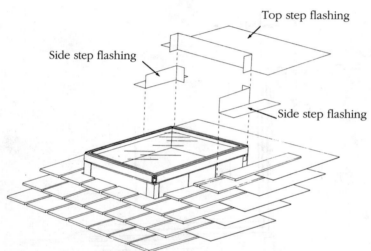

13-27. Side pieces have vertical sections that fold around top corners.
Pella/Rolscreen Co.

A properly-installed skylight will give years of leak-proof service. FIG-URE 13-28 shows your finished installation.

Two or more skylights may be installed in gangs or clusters. You can maintain the structural strength of the roof by selecting units to fit between the rafters, as seen in FIG. 13-2. This eliminates the need to cut and reinforce rafters.

SELF-FLASHING SKYLIGHTS

Self-flashing skylights install directly on a pitched roof. Installation without a curb gives the unit a low profile that makes it less conspicuous. FIG. 13-29 shows this type installation.

13-28. The completed installation.

Locating, marking, and cutting a self-flashing skylight is the same as for a curb-mounted unit. Place the dome in a ¼-inch-thick bead of roofing cement and nail in predrilled holes. Most units come with special nails and rubber washers to secure the skylight in place. Apply a thick coat of roofing cement over the edge of the skylight up to the bubble. Cut strips

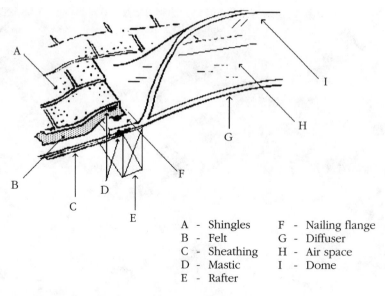

A - Shingles   F - Nailing flange
B - Felt   G - Diffuser
C - Sheathing   H - Air space
D - Mastic   I - Dome
E - Rafter

13-29. Self-flashing skylight.

of roofing felt wide enough to go from the bubble to overlap the felt on deck. Put the side pieces on first, and apply more cement over these strips at the top. Apply the top strips of felt. Don't put a strip at the bottom (see FIG. 13-30).

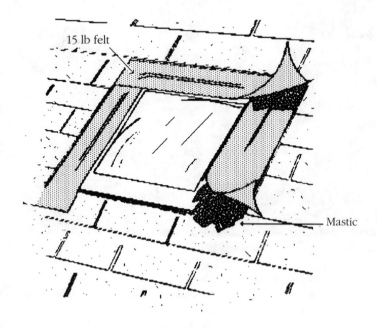

15 lb felt

Mastic

13-30. Applying mastic and felt.

Apply mastic over the felt strips and replace the asphalt shingles. After the shingles are in place, apply roofing cement across the bottom of the skylight. Figure 13-31 shows a cross view of the installation.

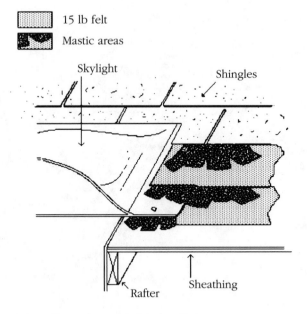

13-31. Cross-view of skylight installation.

Index

moldings (*cont.*)
  finishes used on moldings, 73
  interior walls, 33
  mitering corners and joints, 72
  splicing molding, 72, 73

N

nails
  blued nails, 31
  bright nails, 31
  cement-coated nails, 31
  galvanized nails, 31
  interior wall sizes, types, selection, 30
  per-pound numbers, 30
  phosphate-coated nails, 31
  sizes, types, selection, 30
  wallboard (drywall) nail
    recommendations, 36

P

paneling, 14, 41-43
  adhesives and glues, 43
  "curing" newly delivered panels, 42
  cutouts for outlets, switches, etc., 43
  grain/pattern matching, 42
  labor hours, 45
  materials estimates, 43, 44
  measuring and cutting panels, 42-43
  nailing paneling, 43
  window cutouts, 43
partition walls (*see* walls,interior)
permits, 2-3
plaster walls, 14

R

R-values, insulation, 134-135
rafters (*see* dormers, rafters)
roofs (*see also* dormers; skylights)
  dormers (*see* dormers)
  flashing, 108-113
  labor hours, 113-114
  materials estimates, 113-114
  shingling, 108-113
  truss construction, 11, 12

S

Sheetrock (*see* wallboard
  construction)
skylights (*see also* ceilings; windows),
    227-247
  attic conversions, 176-177
  flashing
    counterflashing installation, 237-239
    self-flashing skylights, 244-247
    step flashing with wood shingles,
      239-244

installation steps, 231-236
insulation of skylight shaft, 230
locating the skylight, 233-234
pitch of roof requirements, 227-228
rafter locations, 228
reinforcing roof, 234
rubber boot installation, 236
selection of skylight, 227-228
setting and installing skylight, 234-236
shafts, framing the skylight shaft,
    228-230
shingling around skylight, 236
wiring, plumbing, etc., 233
sleeper joists, basement floors, 79
sole plates, interior walls, 11, 26, 27
stairways and steps, 205-226
  attic conversions, 216
  boxing in basement stairs, 156-157
  carriages, 214
  carriages, layout, 220-224
  closed- vs. open-string stairs, 208
  concrete basement steps, 142-143
  framing stairways, 218-220
  handrails, balusters, newel posts, 207
  headroom calculations, 207, 213
  labor hours, 225-226
  landings, 210
  laying out stair carriage, 220-224
  locating the stairway, 208
  materials estimates, 225-226
  rise and run calculations, 206-207,
    216-218
  straight and platform stairs, 208, 210
  stringers, 213-215
  terms used in stair construction, 206-
    208
  tread and riser dimensions, 216-218
  types of stairways, 208
  width of stairways, 213
  winders, 220-213
sump pumps, 137
suspended ceilings (*see* ceilings)

T

tile
  ceramic tile flooring, 88
  vinyl tile flooring, 86-87
top plates, interior walls, 14, 26, 27
trusses, roof, 11, 12

V

vapor barriers, 127, 132-133
vinyl sheet flooring, 82-86
  one-piece installation, 84-85
  two-piece installation, 85-86